DELEGATE

The
Key To
Successful
Management

Other Books by the Author

Making Time Work For You (Beaufort Books, 1981)

Managing Your Memory (Beaufort Books, 1982)

Personal Organization: The Key to Managing Your Time
and Your Life (Time Management Consultants, Inc., 1983)

4

DELEGATE

The Key to. Successful Management

Harold L. Taylor

Beaufort Books
New York   Toronto

LIBRARY OF CONGRESS CATALOGUING IN PUBLICATION DATA
Taylor, Harold L.
   Delegate: the key to successful management.
   1. Delegation of authority.   I. Title.
HD50.T39 1984   658.4'02   83-22525
ISBN 0-8253-0190-4

Published in the United States by
Beaufort Books
9 East 40th Street
New York, New York
10016

Published simultaneously in Canada by General Publishing Co. Ltd.

Printed and bound in Canada by John Deyell Company

To Joan Milne —
An extraordinary delegatee

CONTENTS

Chapter 1   14

LEADERSHIP AND DELEGATION

What makes an effective leader. What delegation really is, and why it is essential to effective management. How delegation benefits employees, managers and organizations.

Chapter 2   24

WHY MANAGERS DON'T DELEGATE

How to determine whether you are delegating properly. The reasons managers fail to delegate, and the fallacies of those reasons.

Chapter 3   34

PREPARING TO DELEGATE

Where to start once you have decided to delegate. The various activities that managers are involved in.

Chapter 4   44

FINDING THE TIME TO DELEGATE

Lack of time is the major stumbling block for most managers. How to organize your work and yourself in order to get the time necessary for effective delegation.

Chapter 5   62

THE DELEGATION PROCESS

Analyzing your job and deciding which activities to delegate. Choosing the delegatees and drawing up assignments. Balancing the workload and clarifying responsibility. How to communicate effectively.

Chapter 6   72

RELEASING YOUR JOB TO OTHERS

The hardest part of delegation is letting go. How to ease out of the jobs while your employees take a firm grip on them. Allowing your employees to excel.

Chapter 7   78

GUIDELINES FOR DELEGATION

A summary of the important principals to keep in mind when delegating. How to ensure success during the delegation process.

Chapter 8   88

KEEPING TRACK OF ASSIGNMENTS

How to develop, maintain and use a "Delegation Record" to ensure assignments are completed on time. The "Assignment and Information Record."

Chapter 9   98

CONTROLLING PERFORMANCE

How to communicate *after* your delegation has taken place. Getting maximum performance from your employees. Conducting performance appraisals.

Chapter 10   108

DEVELOPING YOUR PEOPLE

How to maintain a bank of qualified people to assume greater responsibilities. Developing strength within the organization.

Chapter 11   114

ADVICE FOR THE DELEGATEE

What to do if *your* boss won't delegate. Planning your career path. How to develop yourself through study, experience and networking.

Chapter 12   122

DELEGATE OR STAGNATE

How delegation is gaining in importance. Why effective delegation is the key to a successful future in management.

LIST
OF
EXHIBITS

EXHIBIT 1   38

A manager's job, consisting of priorities, time obligations, desirable activities and timewasters.

EXHIBIT 2   39

A manager's job, with the various activities separated.

EXHIBIT 3   40

Activities included in a manager's life.

EXHIBIT 4   41, 42

Pinpoint your timewasters.

EXHIBIT 5   47

Follow-up File System

EXHIBIT 6   50

The Personal Organizer

EXHIBIT 7   51

Telephone & Visitors Log

EXHIBIT 8   53

Telephone Directory

EXHIBIT 9   57
Decisions vs. Time

EXHIBIT 10   60
How to manage people with respect to time.

EXHIBIT 11   64
Activity Analysis

EXHIBIT 12   68
Delegation Assignment Sheet

EXHIBIT 13   90, 91
Delegation Record

EXHIBIT 14   95
Assignment and Information Record

EXHIBIT 15   101
Weekly Communication Record

DELEGATE

The
Key To
Successful
Management

Chapter One

LEADERSHIP and DELEGATION

What Is A Leader?

Leadership is *not* the process of accomplishing great things by ourselves, while gaining the respect of our employees. It is rather the process of accomplishing great things *through our employees*, thereby raising *their* self-respect. Leadership also involves more than simply overseeing or directing others. It involves developing employees' skills through delegation.

A leader must identify an employee's special abilities and make use of them. But he or she must also identify the weak areas and limitations of employees and be willing to help strengthen them. Managers who place a priority on developing their own skills and abilities while ignoring the needs of their employees are not usually effective leaders. In one way, a leader is not a superior. Leaders should not consider themselves superiors in respect to attitude, but only in respect to their position in the organization's hierarchy. Positional power gives the manager the right to give orders; however, it's the personal power earned by being considerate to and respectful of others that gives him or her the right to expect those orders to be carried out effectively. A leader's job is to continually develop the people who report to him or her to such an extent that they could eventually perform delegated tasks better than the leader.

For many managers, this necessitates a change in philosophy. Our natural tendency is to make *ourselves* look good, not others. But an effective leader's goal is to make the employees look *better*. In actual fact, what will happen is that the better your employees become, the better *you* will look. After all, they report to you — and if they're that good, think how good *you* must be.

It takes self-confidence to be an effective leader. There's an element of personal risk in accepting the bulk of the blame for a job poorly done when, in fact, it is another person's error. It takes self-confidence to pass along praise to your employees when the temptation is to soak up some of the credit yourself. But a leader's job is to *lead*, not *do*. Leaders are evaluated on the basis of how well they *lead*. Leadership is accomplishing great things through continually developing the skills and abilities of the people being led.

And this is impossible without delegation.

WHAT IS DELEGATION?

The problem with delegation is that we spend too much time *defining* it and not enough time *doing* it. Suffice it to say that delegation is the process of turning work over to a subordinate. The key word is *process*. It does not mean dumping work onto someone without prior training or guidelines, or constantly delegating to the same employee. Nor does it mean always assigning all the boring, meaningless tasks. The *process* of delegation is what this book is all about.

The work that is turned over is work that is within a manager's area of responsibility. Otherwise, he or she would be in no position to delegate it. And although, in so doing, the manager holds the subordinate *responsible* for its successful completion, and *accountable* for the results, the ultimate responsibility still rests with the manager, and he or she is held accountable by his or her boss in turn.

For the purposes of this book, "delegated work" and "assignments" are considered to be essentially the same thing, but with these differences: assignments may require less of an employee's time, a lesser degree of training and the granting of little authority (or perhaps none at all).

As a manager, how much authority should you delegate to your supervisors? Obviously as much as needed in order to carry out the assigned responsibility. Assigning or delegating responsibility without the necessary authority is not delegation at all since the tasks at hand could not be carried out.

You cannot hold a supervisor or manager responsible for the efficient operation of a manufacturing facility without the authority to hire and fire personnel, change methods, and spend money. You cannot hold a person responsible for improving the appearance of a newsletter without the authority to choose the type, pick colors, and revise the layout. You cannot assign the responsibility for organizing a staff luncheon without the authority to choose a menu and arrange the seating plan. You must delegate the amount of authority needed to carry out the responsibility assigned. There is nothing as frustrating for a manager — and as damaging to an organization — as being assigned responsibility with insufficient authority to carry it out. This produces a situation where the employee is continually running to his or her boss for further direction.

Of course, there must be limitations to the authority granted. Perhaps the plant manager cannot expand the plant facilities, the public relations supervisor cannot change the editorial theme, and the office manager cannot hold the staff meeting in Hawaii. These limits of authority must be spelled out in advance.

The more authority a supervisor has, the less involvement is required on the part of the manager, and consequently the more time he or she will have in order to fulfil managerial responsibilities — particularly those most often neglected due to a lack of time, such as planning, training, goal-setting, and innovation.

Conversely, the more authority a supervisor has, the greater the impact on company profits if he or she makes a mistake. And therein lies the hang-up. Managers are reluctant to turn the wheel over to a new driver if their own safety is at stake. And yet no one can improve their ability to drive *without driving*. The risk is reduced by adequate training, but there will always be a risk. It takes courage to delegate. It takes a willingness to make oneself vulnerable. But successful companies are built by individuals willing to take risks.

Don't be afraid to share your authority with the people you are training. Have as much confidence in them as you would like *your* boss to have in *you*.

THE BENEFITS OF DELEGATION

Delegation is not easy. It requires time, effort and motivation. If you are not convinced that there are benefits to delegation, you won't be motivated to put forth the effort. Here are some major advantages for your consideration.

Releases Time for Managing

The lack of delegation not only develops tunnel vision, it physically prevents managers from performing the functions they were hired to carry out. Managers should be planning, organizing, staffing, directing, controlling and innovating. Instead, they are frequently involved in doing trivial jobs, fighting fires, responding to interruptions and correcting errors made by others.

Managers who delegate have more time to fulfil their responsibilities and develop their own skills, and as a result are more valuable to the company. Delegation is the most important part of being a manager.

Relieves Pressures

Most managers are action-oriented. They prefer to be in the thick of things, doing instead of supervising.

Lack of delegation allows this tendency to get out of hand. Managers are involved in so many activities that the pressure of having too many jobs and too little time keeps them constantly harried and hassled. This can result in ulcers, heart problems, nervous breakdowns, high blood pressure and other stress-induced problems. It makes them less effective and they are perceived by *their* managers to be disorganized, and out of control.

Delegation, once mastered, relieves time pressures. And the manager is able to control the job instead of the job controlling him or her.

Develops People

Delegation provides employees with the opportunity to grow — to expand their skills and decision-making capability. It allows them to accept greater responsibility gradually, in a non-threatening environment, preparing them for further advancement. It encourages them to be creative, and to put what talents they already have toward practicing their problem-solving skills.

No amount of education or off-the-job training can develop an employee more quickly, thoroughly and effectively than practical experience. People learn by doing. And delegation provides that opportunity.

Provides a Motivational Climate

Motivation is simply helping others become what they are capable of becoming. Since delegation requires knowing the employee's personal goals, abilities and desires, the manager is better able to provide the opportunity for individuals to excel in areas that satisfy their particular needs.

Since delegation forces managers to spend time with their subordinates, it also tends to improve interpersonal relationships because most people require encouragement in order to excel. They crave attention. Those who claim they would rather be left alone and contacted only when they make errors are in the minority. People need the constant feedback and consistent reinforcement that tells them they are doing okay. The process of delegation provides that constant contact which reaffirms the employee's value as an individual.

Provides Performance Standards

Without delegation, managers normally evaluate their employees based on activity rather than results. By delegating specific tasks and responsibilities along with the necessary authority to carry them out, the manager can evaluate an employee based on actual *accomplishments*. Evaluation becomes meaningful, and compensation can be tied to merit rather than busyness.

Increases Results

Effective time use is that which is devoted to move the organization towards the attainment of its goals. These goals are normally reflected outside an organization, i.e. the attainment of profits, the provision of a service, etc. So managers must think outwards and not be so preoccupied with internal activities as to lose sight of the real goals. Preoccupation with internal procedures tends to breed *efficiency*, not *effectiveness*. Instead of first seeking better methods of processing paperwork, recording statistics or producing a product, there should be a constant barrage of questions: "Is this paperwork necessary?" "Do these statistics contribute to the attainment of the goal?" "Is this particular product the best one in relation to the goal we are attempting to achieve?" Effective thinking is results-oriented thinking, and results-oriented thinking must encompass the organization as a whole.

Unfortunately, managers are frequently too busy *doing* the tasks at hand to question their necessity and impact on organizational goals. Delegation releases managers from the tyranny of activity and elevates them to a level where they can assess the effect of activity on organizational goals. Delegation extends the results that managers can obtain — from what they can do personally to what they can direct others to do.

Develops the Organization

Delegation makes the fullest use of an organization's personnel. While lack of delegation stifles initiative, encouraging the process allows every employee to excel, and to devote his or her talents, skills and innovative ability to the good of the organization.

Every individual is unique. Each one has different experiences to draw upon. Having those experiences as an available resource, rather than stifled by an autocratic manager, can only strengthen the organization. Delegation develops people who are able to work independently with a minimum of direction. And these are the easiest kind of people to supervise.

Delegation also ensures that qualified people are available for promotion to fill vacancies. Through delegation, managers are able to develop their own replacements, thereby making their own advancement possible.

Chapter Two

WHY MANAGERS DON'T DELEGATE

Indicators of Ineffective Delegation

There's no greater timesaver than effective delegation. It frees up some of your time so you can concentrate on important, meaningful activities. Unfortunately, some people *think* they are delegating when, actually, they are simply handing out assignments. Some people "dump" jobs onto their subordinates without sufficient training or follow-up. What are the indicators of improper delegation? Here are twenty-five of them. If you can answer "yes" to several of these statements, there's a good chance *you* are not delegating effectively.

I have a good idea of what I
want to accomplish but I don't
seem to be getting anywhere.   YES ____ NO ____

I always seem to be giving
orders of one kind or another.   YES ____ NO ____

I'm always checking up on my
people to make sure they're
carrying out their assigned
tasks properly.   YES ____ NO ____

I leave my people alone. If they
have problems, they can always
contact me. Otherwise I assume
everything is going okay.   YES ____ NO ____

I take a lot of work home
evenings and weekends.   YES ____ NO ____

I work under constant pressure.
And when I'm away from the
office, jobs tend to pile up.   YES ____ NO ____

I tend to be very critical of my subordinates. YES ____ NO ____

I don't really have any policies to guide my people. If they're in doubt about anything, they can call me. YES ____ NO ____

My people feel restricted by the policies, procedures and rules I issue. YES ____ NO ____

My people don't really understand my objectives and they don't have clear objectives for themselves. YES ____ NO ____

My people are slow or reluctant to make decisions on their own. I have to make too many decisions for them. YES ____ NO ____

When I'm away from the office, I call frequently. YES ____ NO ____

I try to limit my span of control so I can keep tabs on everyone. YES ____ NO ____

I don't encourage my subordinates to participate in meetings with contacts at higher levels even when the subject falls within their own area of competence. I like to do that myself. YES ____ NO ____

My people don't have the authority to purchase items without my approval. YES ____ NO ____

I tend to give orders in my
boss's name rather than my
own.   YES ____ NO ____

I get so bogged down in details
of the jobs below me that I don't
have enough time for organizing,
directing and controlling.   YES ____ NO ____

All tasks are equally important
so I don't bother setting
priorities when making
assignments.   YES ____ NO ____

I'm always getting partially
completed projects from my
people. No one seems to finish
anything without checking with
me first.   YES ____ NO ____

One of my biggest timewasters
is continual interruptions by my
employees.   YES ____ NO ____

I don't have any qualified
subordinates who could replace
me if I were promoted.   YES ____ NO ____

Every day seems to bring a
series of crises or emergencies
that I have to handle.   YES ____ NO ____

I really can't afford to take a
long vacation or an extended
leave of absence because the
place would fall apart.   YES ____ NO ____

I believe if you want something
done right, you've got to do it
yourself.   YES ____ NO ____

By the time I put in a week at
this job, I'm just too exhausted
to go anywhere with my family
on the weekends.   YES ____ NO ____

If you are not delegating effectively, you must first
determine the reasons. There are certainly grounds
for not delegating everything. Perhaps an activity can
only be carried out by a manager at your level in the
organization. Perhaps it involves confidential information. Perhaps it is a personal responsibility such as
conducting performance appraisals, disciplining — or
hiring or firing.

But, in the majority of cases, the lack of delegation
is simply due to a reluctance to delegate.

THE "DO IT YOURSELF" SYNDROME

Doing something yourself is rarely justified unless it's
unique to your position or yourself. If you are a manager, with people reporting to you, your goal should
be to delegate as much as possible. Assuming you
receive a higher salary than your subordinates, you
simply can't afford yourself! And a manager's job is to
get things done through other people, not to do the
work himself.

If delegation is such an ideal way of developing
subordinates while freeing the manager to work on

priorities, why is there such a reluctance to delegate? Here are some common excuses, and a comment or two about the fallacy of each.

There's no time to delegate.

A common excuse, since delegation requires training and training takes time. It's faster to do a job than to train someone else to do it. It makes sense if it's a once-in-a-lifetime job. But if the task is repetitive, there's a break-even point at which the amount of time spent training personnel equals the total time saved by having the task done by someone else. And from then on it's all savings.

I can do the job better than anyone else.

Of course you can; after all, look how often you've done it! But with training and experience, your subordinate will be able to do it just as well, or better. In the meantime, you will have to accept something less than perfect. Compare the job they do with the job you *used to do* when you started umpteen years ago. Don't compare it to your *current* performance.

I enjoy doing it.

Good. Think how much your employees may enjoy doing it! Nothing motivates more than a challenging and interesting task. And you will be able to take on even more interesting, challenging and profitable tasks in turn.

It's company policy.

A policy is a guideline, not a rule. Job descriptions aren't carved in stone. Change the policy or job description if necessary. People should control policies; policies shouldn't control people.

It's a force of habit.

Quite likely. The more frequently you do something, the more habitual it becomes. But habits can be broken when you consciously set your mind to do so. Form a *new* habit of sitting down with your subordinate for fifteen minutes every day to train him or her to do the job.

My employees aren't capable.

Don't sell them short. Is your opinion based on their present performance or what they could do with some good, consistent training? Someone once showed confidence in you; show confidence in others in return.

My people are too busy to take on more jobs.

No doubt. But what are they busy *at*? Are there some low pay-off jobs that can be eliminated without any detrimental impact on company goals? Your employees should be working on important, essential tasks, not those that are "nice to have done."

If I delegate too much, my job could be threatened.

If you delegate too *little*, your job could be lost! And don't kid yourself. If your employees do a good job, it makes *you* look good. If other people are able to take over your job, you are promotable. So help them take over your job by delegating to them.

My boss may think I'm lazy.

If you don't delegate, he or she will *know* you're lazy! Doing a familiar job only takes time; training another person to do the job takes effort.

My boss told me to do it.

Are you sure the boss didn't tell you to *get it done.* A manager's responsibilities exceed his or her capacity to do them personally. Managers can only fulfil their bosses' expectations through delegation.

I'm afraid of losing control.

You won't lose control if you explain your subordinate's limit of authority and insist on feedback. You're delegating, not abdicating. You are still ultimately responsible for the jobs you delegate.

I haven't the heart to dump jobs onto somebody else.

Amazing how we don't have such consideration for ourselves! You're not dumping, you're delegating — which involves an assessment of your employees' current workload, and a determination of what can be eliminated, simplified or reassigned.

Doing it myself gives me a high profile.

It also gives you high blood pressure. There's even more prestige in delegating a prestigious task, so don't hang on to jobs just for the recognition.

I want to keep busy.

How about running up a "down" escalator; it's better for cardiovascular fitness. Workaholics are poor delegators and usually ineffective managers.

My employees would complain if I gave them more work to do.

You're not giving them *more* work, you're giving them *better* work. And when's the last time you discussed it with them? The only way to discover your employees' aspirations is to talk to them. If you have dead-end people, match them up with dead-end jobs. But make sure what they *are* doing is important. Not everyone aspires to the presidency. But they can still be valuable to the organization in a position which affords no opportunity for further promotion.

My employees don't have the information at hand to make decisions.

Can you give it to them? Or is the information exclusive to your level in the organization? If so, it could very well be that the task shouldn't be delegated. Some jobs, such as those that are confidential or personal in nature, have to be retained by yourself.

Question *your* reasons for not delegating. Are they legitimate? Or are they simply rationalizations for maintaining the status quo?

Chapter Three

PREPARING TO DELEGATE

Examine Your Activities

If you are typical of most managers, you are too busy to actually sit down and categorize the kinds of activities you are involved in. But if you were to examine them, they could be distinguished as follows:

Priorities

These are the important activities which contribute directly to the attainment of your personal and company's goals. They are key tasks which would take only about 20 percent of your time to yield about 80 percent of your results. They could include planning, motivating and evaluating employees, delegating, goal setting, professional development, self-renewal, and maintaining important business contacts. Those activities falling within a manager's area of responsibility, such as planning, organizing, staffing, directing, controlling, innovating, and representing are included as "Priorities." They are normally long-term as opposed to urgent and may fall victim to procrastination while you concentrate on immediate — and less important — concerns.

Lack of effectiveness on the part of managers can usually be attributed to insufficient time being devoted to the priority activities. And this lack of time is a result of the time demands made by activities from the following categories.

Time Obligations

These are relatively important activities that do contribute to the attainment of goals, but are not nearly as important as the priorities. Most meetings, telephone calls, business trips, correspondence, reports and reading materials fall into this category. Very few organizations could survive without occasionally

holding meetings, or writing reports. They are necessary, but not generally critical. And they usually
mean much wasted time. In fact, these are the activities which receive most of the blame for a manager's
time problems. Yet such is not the case. Spending time
on the unnecessary activities, mentioned later, is
where time problems occur.

Managers probably spend about 40 to 45 percent of
their time on this category of activities.

Desirable Activities

These activities are useful, and performing them
makes a work environment more pleasant. For example, it's not essential that the windows be cleaned, the
files thinned out, the walls painted or the coffee made.
But it is certainly desirable to have these done. However, these activities are not as important as time
obligations, and the consequences of performing them
poorly are not as great.

These desirable, but relatively unimportant activities, probably consume about 10 to 15 percent of a
manager's time.

Timewasters

These are trivial, unimportant activities which contribute absolutely nothing to the attainment of personal or company goals. An estimated 10 to 15 percent
of a manager's job is spent wheelspinning — searching for misplaced items, shuffling papers, enduring
interruptions, backtracking due to forgetfulness, pro-
crastinating are just a few examples of the dozens of
ways a manager wastes time. Most of these time-
wasting activities are the result of personal disorgani-
zation. These activities are unimportant, undesirable,

and *unwanted*. Also included in this category are activities which are obsolete or redundant: reports that are no longer needed, committee meetings held when the committee's objective has already been reached, procedures being followed which no longer match the job, and correspondence being generated which serves no useful purpose.

Exhibit 1 shows these various activities intermingled. Seldom do managers stop long enough to analyze their jobs, and categorize the various activities. If they did, they would find that only a small percentage of their total time was being consumed by the important activities (see Exhibit 2). Unfortunately, this is not how it *should* be. The timewasters should be eliminated completely. The desirable activities and many of the time obligations should be delegated to others. This would leave more time for those key activities which produce the majority of the results.

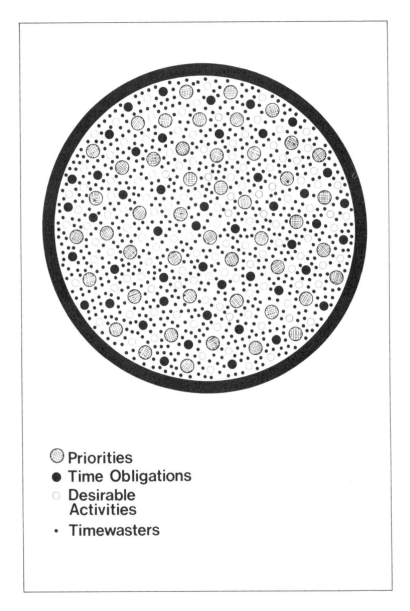

- ⊕ Priorities
- ● Time Obligations
- ○ Desirable Activities
- · Timewasters

EXHIBIT 1

A manager's job, consisting of priorities, time obligations, desirable activities and timewasters.

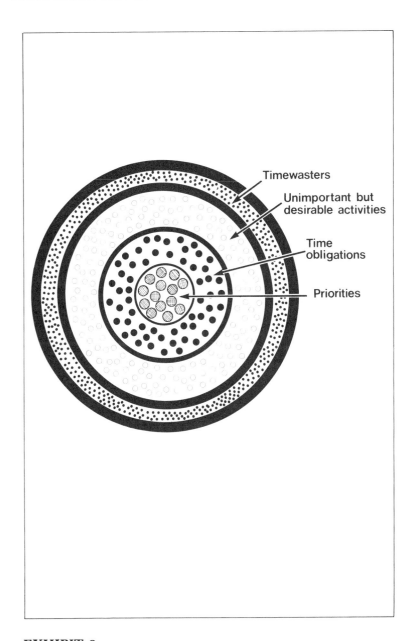

EXHIBIT 2

A manager's job, with the various activities separated.

Time Wasters	Time Obligations	Priorities
Procrastination	Travel	Goal Setting
Forgetting Things	Reading	Planning
Searching for Lost Items	Visitors	Delegation
Shuffling Papers	Boss	Training
Perfectionism	Correspondence	Self-Development
Indecision	Commuting	Creativity
Upward Delegation	Telephone	Self-Renewal
Idle Time	Interruptions	Organizing
Self-Interruptions	Meetings	Family Activities
Inability to say "No"	Crises	
Worry	Mail	
Not Listening		

EXHIBIT 3

Activities included in a manager's life.

PINPOINT YOUR TIME WASTERS

The first step in effective time management is to recognize that we are the ones primarily responsible for our own time problems — not the other people. By managing ourselves more effectively with respect to time, we can greatly increase our accomplishments within a given time frame.

If you are not satisfied with what you are now able to accomplish in the time available, determine which of the following time wasters are applicable to yourself. They are all within your control.

Once you have pinpointed those time wasters which seem to apply to your situation, set up a plan to systematically reduce their effect.

- ☐ LACK OF DELEGATION
- ☐ PROCRASTINATION
- ☐ LACK OF PLANNING, SCHEDULING, ORGANIZATION
- ☐ TROUBLE GETTING STARTED IN MORNINGS
- ☐ OVER-EXTENDED COFFEE BREAKS & LUNCHES
- ☐ IDLE TIME, TALK, DAYDREAMING
- ☐ SORTING & DISPENSING WITH MAIL
- ☐ SEARCHING FOR FILES, INFORMATION
- ☐ READING MAGAZINES, JUNK MAIL
- ☐ SHUFFLING PAPERS
- ☐ PROOFREADING AND SIGNING LETTERS
- ☐ CONSTANT CHECKING ON EMPLOYEES
- ☐ SPENDING TIME ON NON-PRIORITY ITEMS
- ☐ INTER-OFFICE TRAVEL
- ☐ TOO LONG ON TELEPHONE
- ☐ RE-WRITING MEMOS & LETTERS
- ☐ MARTINI LUNCHES
- ☐ LACK OF WRITTEN GOALS
- ☐ INABILITY TO SAY "NO"
- ☐ HOLDING UNNECESSARY MEETINGS
- ☐ POOR CONTROL OF MEETINGS
- ☐ RELYING ON MENTAL NOTES
- ☐ DELAYING DISTASTEFUL TASKS
- ☐ NO "QUIET HOUR"

EXHIBIT 4

Pinpoint your timewasters.

- ☐ NOT USING PRIME TIME FOR PRIORITY WORK
- ☐ NOT UTILIZING WAITING TIME AND TRAVEL TIME
- ☐ FILING TOO MUCH, THROWING OUT TOO LITTLE
- ☐ SELF-INTERRUPTIONS
- ☐ NOT UTILIZING FORMS
- ☐ INDECISION
- ☐ ALLOWING CONSTANT INTERRUPTIONS BY OTHERS
- ☐ WRITING INSTEAD OF 'PHONING
- ☐ INEFFICIENT OFFICE LAYOUT
- ☐ INSISTING ON KNOWING ALL AND SEEING ALL
- ☐ NOT KEEPING SECRETARY/ASSISTANT ADVISED OF APPOINTMENTS, MEETINGS
- ☐ NOT HAVING FACTS, TELEPHONE NUMBERS, AT HAND
- ☐ UNCLEAR COMMUNICATIONS
- ☐ NOT TAKING ADVANTAGE OF TIME-SAVING GADGETS
- ☐ TOO MUCH ATTENTION TO DETAIL; PERFECTIONISM
- ☐ NO DAILY PLAN
- ☐ NO SELF-IMPOSED DEADLINES
- ☐ LEAVING TASKS UNFINISHED & STARTING NEW ONES
- ☐ ALLOWING UPWARD DELEGATION
- ☐ DOING OTHER PEOPLE'S WORK
- ☐ NOT EFFECTIVELY TRAINING STAFF
- ☐ FIREFIGHTING
- ☐ PREOCCUPATION WITH PROBLEMS
- ☐ NO FOLLOW-UP SYSTEM
- ☐ NOT ACTIVELY LISTENING
- ☐ TOO MUCH TIME ON PERSONAL & OUTSIDE ACTIVITIES
- ☐ POOR ATTITUDE TOWARD THE JOB
- ☐ WORRY, LACK OF CONFIDENCE
- ☐ LACK OF PROCEDURES
- ☐ FAILURE TO USE DICTATION EQUIPMENT
- ☐ POOR WRITING SKILLS
- ☐ ABSENTMINDEDNESS

Chapter Four

FINDING THE TIME TO DELEGATE

Get Organized

Delegation is a great way to ease the load but, if you delegate when you're snowed under with work, you'll probably do a poor job of it. You will be forced to dump jobs onto others, as though in desperation, without sufficient time to plan and train. The errors that could be made by your employees may take longer to correct than the time you had hoped to save through delegating. Even worse, you'll lose confidence in your employees' abilities and will shy away from delegating important activities to them in the future.

Instead, schedule blocks of time in your planning calendar well in advance and make delegation a *gradual* process. Recognize that employees must be trained, and that delegation takes an *investment* of more time on your part. In order to get that time you may have to take some drastic measures like eliminating unessential tasks, saying "no" more frequently, making yourself unavailable at certain times of the day, and getting yourself organized.

Don't ever say you don't have enough time to delegate. You have all the time there is to have — twenty-four hours every single day for the rest of your life. If you feel pressured, or can't seem to accomplish everything you want to accomplish, you had better take a close look at how you spend that time.

To reiterate, there are four categories of activities that fill your twenty-four hours. "Timewasters" are within your control, and contribute nothing toward your goals. "Desirable" activities are those that are useful but not really essential. "Time obligations" are those necessary yet relatively unimportant activities that form a part of your job. "Priorities" are those key activities which are responsible for most of your results. They lead you directly to your goals.

Since your goals may differ from the next person's, your priorities may also differ. The same holds true for the timewasters and time obligations. "Interruptions" may be a timewaster for a scientist, but are integral to the activities of a sales clerk. Similarly, telephone calls may be time obligations for managers, but priority activities for telephone answering service personnel.

It is imperative, therefore, that you set goals and know exactly where you're heading. But this is not necessarily the place to start. If you are like most people, you just don't have time to set goals. In fact, you probably don't have enough time for any of the priority activities, including delegation.

So the place to start is to eliminate the bulk of the timewasters — those caused by lack of personal organization. Do this by cleaning up your work area, organizing your files, developing a system of handling your mail, and maintaining a "personal organizer" to reduce the problems associated with forgetfulness, follow-ups, interruptions and searching for information.

Once you are organized, eliminate as many other timewasters and desirable activities as possible, then reduce the time spent on time obligations. As a result you will have enough time to spend on the real priorities, one of the top priorities being delegation itself.

From then on, it's a continual process of managing yourself with respect to time, concentrating on the priorities and gradually eliminating more of the time-wasters in your life.

Keep Your Desk Clean

You work more effectively with a clear desk. Papers, reports, magazines and miscellaneous clutter distract you from the job at hand. Your eyes light on a stack of correspondence and your brain does a double take as it thinks about all those unanswered letters. Dispense with correspondence daily. Use follow-up files, pro-

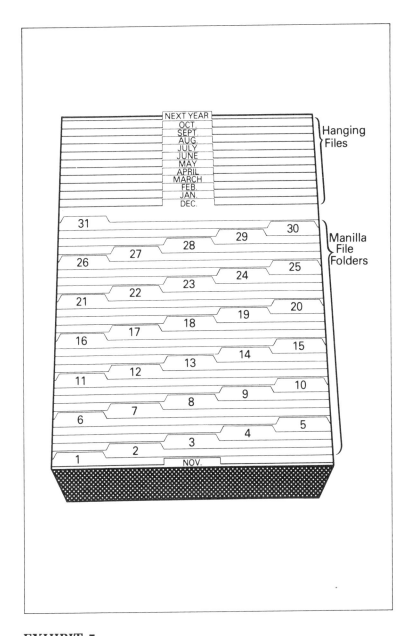

EXHIBIT 5

Follow-up File System

ject files, idea files. Reserve time daily for dispensing with paperwork. Keep your desk clear by organizing your office environment, your systems and yourself.

Ideally, your desk should be cleared every night before going home except for the project you want to begin the next morning. It may sound unrealistic, but it's a goal to aim for. Psychologists claim we enjoy our evening and weekend pursuits a lot more when we leave the office with an organized desk and a plan for the next day.

Keep your desk out of sight of the doorway to avoid distractions. Keep frequently used files within easy reach, but keep them out of sight when you are not actually working on them. Have a spot for everything and don't vary it. Know exactly where to reach for your telephone, dictation unit, day planner, paper-clips, staples and pens.

Use Follow-Up Files

A follow-up system helps keep us organized. It gets paperwork off our desks, forces us to schedule tasks for specific dates, and prevents us from forgetting follow-ups and deadlines.

But before you make one up, be sure that you're going to use it! It's a time management tool to increase your effectiveness. When you put something in your follow-up file, you are scheduling it to be done on a specific date. If it's a task that will take more than a few minutes, you must schedule that time in your planning diary as you put it in the follow-up file. Then it will not be necessary to re-schedule it due to lack of time.

One simple follow-up file system requires thirteen hanging files. Mark the tabs with the months of the year. Mark the thirteenth one "Next Year." Then label thirty-one manila folders from 1 to 31 for the days of the month. Place the manila folders in the current month's hanging file. Turn the folders which represent weekends and holidays so they're in backwards. This will prevent you from scheduling tasks and follow-ups on these dates.

Now you're in business. Check your planning diary first thing each morning. If you have a task scheduled, you will know any back-up papers are in the follow-up file under that date. There's no need to keep papers on your desk. Don't re-schedule anything unless absolutely necessary. If it's worth doing at all, it's worth doing *right then* — at the scheduled time.

Personal Organizer

I've developed what I call a "Personal Organizer" which has become my indispensable time management tool. (See Exhibit 6.) It records everything as it occurs and keeps me posted as to what has yet to be done. You will eliminate misplaced messages or telephone numbers and follow-ups that tend to slip your memory. Here are three sections you should include:

Daily Telephone and Visitors Log. This section eliminates the need for those scraps of paper which keep getting misplaced. And it prevents you from ever having to rely on your memory after a visitor has left or a caller has hung up. It consists of a series of simple forms on which you record the caller's name, company, nature of business discussed, and any follow up required. The follow-up section is to the right of the form where it stands out. When the follow-up is completed, the notation in that section is crossed out. By flipping through the pages, you can tell at a glance whether any follow-ups are required. It's a permanent record of any call or visit made or received, and the sheets can eventually be filed away as a diary, or

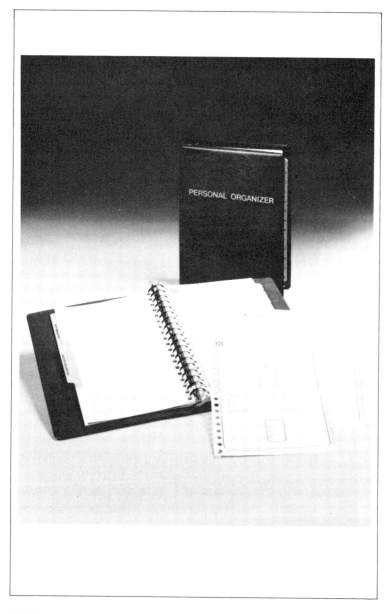

EXHIBIT 6

The Personal Organizer

TELEPHONE & VISITORS LOG

NAME_____ DATE_____

COMPANY_____ TIME_____

NUMBER_____

NATURE OF BUSINESS

CALL ☐
VISIT ☐
INITIATED BY:
MYSELF ☐
OTHER PARTY ☐
TIME: _____

LENGTH
OF
CALL
MINUTES

ACTION REQUIRED

NAME_____ DATE_____

COMPANY_____ TIME_____

NUMBER_____

NATURE OF BUSINESS

CALL ☐
VISIT ☐
INITIATED BY:
MYSELF ☐
OTHER PARTY ☐
TIME: _____

LENGTH
OF
CALL
MINUTES

ACTION REQUIRED

EXHIBIT 7

Telephone & Visitors Log

discarded once any relevant information, such as telephone numbers, has been lifted. It takes only a few seconds to fill out — the same amount of time it takes to scribble on those scraps of paper that get misplaced — but saves hours.

Delegation Record. Ever assign a task or project to someone and then forget to follow up? Then add another series of sheets to that binder — simple forms that describe the tasks, indicate to whom you have delegated them, the due date, and actual completion date. Keep a separate sheet for each person reporting to you. This form will be described fully in Chapter Eight.

Telephone Directory. No need to fumble for your little black book whenever you want to make a call. Just add another section with alphabetical dividers, make up your own name and address forms, and you have your own directory. It's constantly at your fingertips. And the forms can have room for other essential information such as who the person is and physical description, the circumstances of your meeting and so on. Nothing's more frustrating than seeing names in your directory a few years later and wondering who they are. Your directory never fills up or becomes outdated. Simply add or remove pages at will.

Office Layout

Take a look at your office layout. Does the arrangement of desks, files and cabinets match the work flow? Supplies and equipment should be close to the people who use them.

Individuals who frequently deal with one another

TELEPHONE DIRECTORY

NAME — COMPANY — ADDRESS	DESCRIPTION	TELEPHONE NUMBERS
		Business:
		Home:
		Business:
		Home:
		Business:
		Home:
		Business:
		Home:
		Business:
		Home:
		Business:
		Home:
		Business:
		Home:
		Business:
		Home:
		Business:
		Home:
		Business:
		Home:

EXHIBIT 8

Telephone Directory

should be located in the same area. Consider movable files, storage devices, area dividers. Remember, if one person wastes fifteen minutes a day looking for supplies or running back and forth between desks, that's two weeks of lost time per year. So make sure the main office is organized as well.

By organizing yourself, your office and your files, and by adopting effective work habits, you will be able to save a half-hour or more each day. Use this time to meet with your employees on a regular basis to train them to take over parts of your job. Schedule appointments in your planning diary and protect that time from interruptions.

It takes time to delegate. And if you don't have time, you must make time. If you need more help to get organized and reduce the time being spent on the time obligations, I recommend that you read my first book, *Making Time Work For You* (General Publishing/ Beaufort Books, 1981). If your life is riddled with time-consuming habits that you have acquired over the years, I recommend my other time management book, *Personal Organization: The Key to Managing Your Time and Your Life* (Time Management Consultants, Inc., 1983).

Utilize Your Secretary's Time Wisely

Klaus Haider, president of Word Processing International, Ottawa, was quoted in the January, 1983 edition of *The Financial Post* as saying that most secretaries are underutilized and undermotivated. According to the article, his company interviewed thousands of secretaries over a five-year period and concluded that their time is broken up, on average, as follows:

37 percent on administration
25 percent on typing, shorthand and word processing
19 percent of "gofering" — going out for whatever
14 percent on no activity at all
 5 percent on personal, nonproductive office time such as rest periods and coffee breaks

In the same article, Toni Worall, former president of the Toronto chapter of the Association of Administrative Assistants, is quoted as saying, "If a company needs a 'gofer,' it should hire someone specifically for that task."

The article concludes that "the key to improving your secretary's productivity is to make her a part of the office team." This is accomplished through delegation, since most secretaries have greater capacity and ability than their bosses think.

In his book, *The Aggressive Management Style* (Prentice Hall, 1981), Norman Kobert reported that a sampling of over fifty secretaries' activities revealed that almost one-third of their total time was consumed by interruptions to perform "indirect work." This indirect work consisted of such activities as delivering mail, making copies, getting supplies and retrieving lost files. The company in question was in the process of recruiting sixteen new secretaries but, instead, hired six gofers to work for the secretarial group so they could spend most of their time on secretarial work. The program was successful and the company shared the savings with the secretaries.

The moral of this story could be that we could get by with fewer people — whether secretaries, professionals or managers — if all they had to perform were the activities requiring their particular expertise. Do you really need highly skilled professionals plus three or even four assistants in a lower classification? It's an uneconomical use of time to have managers doing the work of secretaries, and secretaries doing the work of filing clerks or mail clerks.

Look at your own job as well. Are you spending one-third of your time doing jobs that a less-skilled person could perform? It's commendable if you feel that no job is beneath you. But can your company really afford to pay you $30 an hour for a $10 an hour job?

Many of us are reluctant to settle for anything less than perfect — whether it be a letter, report, office cleaning or a carwash. But try to remember that by spending unnecessary time on a task, other high pay-off activities may be shortchanged.

Remember also the law of diminishing returns. In a task nearing completion, to achieve perfection may require twice the time that you have already invested in that project. As Exhibit 9 indicates, the more important the task, the more time you can afford to spend on it. Don't waste time on low pay-off activities.

It's interesting to note that managers feel their employees are doing important, necessary work, and yet never so important that it cannot be interrupted or postponed by seemingly minor emergencies. Thus employees are asked to pick up a parcel at customs, drive a visitor to the airport, or run some errands for the boss. Sometimes emergencies may occur where there is no alternative but to interrupt a member of the staff. But practices can become habitual, and are a waste of valuable time as well as an abuse of managerial privilege.

The next time you are tempted to interrupt an employee, ask yourself if there is a less expensive alternative — such as using a courier service or a taxi.

A secretary's greatest timesaver can be the boss. Here are a few more ways to help your secretary become more effective.

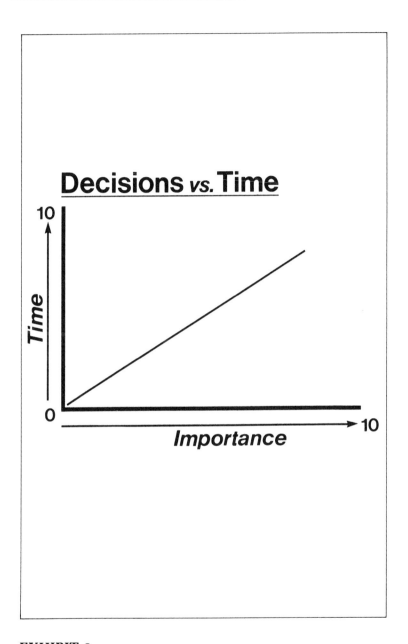

EXHIBIT 9

Decisions vs. Time

1. Delegate challenging and meaningful tasks and encourage your secretary to suggest tasks, reports, procedures which can be eliminated or abbreviated.

2. Make your secretary a part of your management team. A brief five-minute meeting each morning will keep him/her aware of your priorities, appointments and plans.

3. Communicate. A knowledgeable secretary can save you hours of time each week by providing information to callers and visitors without having to disturb you.

4. If you make a business trip or take a vacation, spend some time briefing your secretary on matters that are likely to occur during your absence.

5. Don't be a perfectionist with your secretary. Results are what count. Accept letters and reports that are less than perfect, without sending them back to have the i's dotted and the t's crossed.

6. Provide your secretary with time management tools such as a daily planning diary and follow-up files. Pass along articles on time management. Provide training through seminars and films.

7. Don't keep interrupting with trivial assignments. Accumulate the material in a folder and review the contents with your secretary once per day.

8. Set a good example. Get organized. Plan your day. Give realistic deadlines on typing and other assignments. Don't procrastinate, waste time, or bury yourself in routine tasks. And above all, always respect your secretary's time.

Keep Typists Organized

Do you ever have to follow up with your secretary or typist because you didn't get your letter typed when you wanted it? It's not surprising. Most typists keep all the letters in one folder, and frequently start on the top ones regardless of their importance.

And it's frequently the manager's fault. It's your responsibility to write a desired completion date on every typing job you assign. Never use "A.S.A.P." or "Urgent." A good system is to make up five color folders representing the days in a month. They could be marked as follows:

> First folder 1–6
> Second folder 7–12
> Third folder 13–18
> Fourth folder 19–24
> Fifth folder 25–31

These are to be stored *vertically* in an appropriate holder on the typist's desk.

Whenever you write a letter or report, mark the actual date you need it. (e.g. November 12th). The secretary will put it in the folder marked 7–12 and will complete it during that time period. If you have a great deal of typing, use thirty-one folders, one for every day of the month.

If the typist ends up with too much material scheduled for the same period, you will have to reassess priorities.

If you want to keep a record of the due dates, simply number every letter you write and jot down that number in your planning calendar under the appropriate day. This will not only allow you to follow up,

	How many of these ideas can you use? They're all proven methods of managing yourself effectively with respect to time.	I DO THIS NOW	I'LL TRY THIS	DOES NOT APPLY TO ME
1.	Write out your long-range and short-range goals.			
2	Carry an abbreviated version of your goals with you at all times.			
3.	Every day do something to bring you closer to your lifetime goals.			
4.	Decide what kinds of activities will be done at different times of the day (Time Policy)			
5.	Schedule a "quiet hour" each day.			
6.	Don't let others infringe on your valuable "prime time".			
8.	Set priorities according to importance, not urgency.			
9.	Use your planning calendar to schedule your "to do" list.			
10.	Schedule "appointments with yourself" to complete priority work.			
11.	Use a 'Telephone & Visitors' Log" to keep track of all calls and visits.			
12.	Use a "Delegation Record" to record assignments to others.			
13.	Take advantage of forms, labels and stamps to conserve time.			
14.	Kick the procrastination habit.			
15.	Delegate whenever possible.			
16.	Take advantage of commute and travel time to get things done.			
17.	Have your visitors and telephone calls screened.			
18.	Have majority of mail routed to other people for handling.			
19.	Have your mail separated into "priority" and "routine" before it gets to you.			
20.	Throw out as much correspondence and other paperwork as possible.			
21.	Arrange your office furniture, equipment and files to minimize lost time.			
22.	Use a cassette recorder to dictate memos.			
23.	Delegate the writing of as many reports and memos as possible.			
24.	Don't read your letters before signing them.			
25.	Don't write when a telephone call will do.			

TAYLOR

Harold L. Taylor Enterprises Ltd. 1980

EXHIBIT 10

How to manage people with respect to time.

it will prevent you from scheduling too much typing on any one day.

If you want your employees to manage their time better, you can give them advice, training, ideas, books, time management tools and systems. But *how you conduct yourself* is the greatest training technique of all. What you *are* will have a greater impact than what you *say*. You are the model. Manage your own time effectively, and watch how it catches on!

Chapter Five

THE DELEGATION PROCESS

Deciding What To Delegate

One of the primary steps to take when deciding what to delegate is to do a complete job activity analysis. Draw up a form similar to the one shown in Exhibit 11. In the left-hand column, list all the activities that you perform and decisions you make on a regular basis. Don't leave anything out. If you unlock the office door in the morning, write it down. If you occasionally answer the boss's telephone, write it down. Take a good twenty minutes or half-hour and do nothing but record your activities and recurring decisions. When you're finished, slip the sheet into your top drawer and forget about it for a week. (To prevent forgetting it altogether, scribble a follow-up note on your weekly planning diary.) A week later, take out the sheet, reread it, and start jotting down those other jobs and decisions which will pop into your mind. By this stage you may have written ten or more pages of activities.

Once again, toss the forms into your top drawer and retrieve them about three or four weeks later. Reread the list. Even more items will come to mind — activities that you only perform every few weeks or once per month. And you may still think of more of those insignificant little jobs that take only a few minutes of your time. Include them all. It's the minutes that add up to hours, so include everything.

Next, for each activity, estimate the time it takes each month to perform it, and record that figure in the column to the right of it. This will probably be the first time you have ever thought about the amount of time you are actually spending on the various activities. This gives you an idea of what they are costing you and the company. Is it worth three hours — perhaps $75.00 — to have that monthly summary of product returns? Is it worth $300 to have a "Lates and Absences Report"? These figures will also tell you approximately how much time someone else will have to free up in order to take over these jobs from you.

Next comes the time for honest self-appraisal. Why

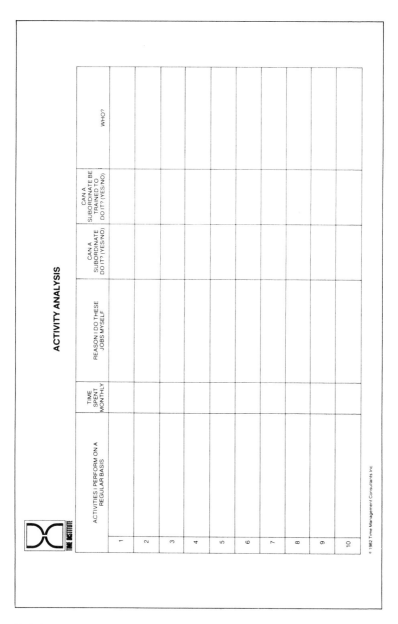

EXHIBIT 11

Activity Analysis

are you doing these jobs yourself? Was your reason discussed in chapter two? Or is there some other reason? Note a reply in the third column to the right of each item. It's at this point that you will be able to judge the category to which the activity belongs. Is it actually a timewaster which contributes nothing to company goals? Can it be eliminated with no detrimental affect on your targets of performance and company objectives? If so, write the word "eliminate" in the column to the far right. Be careful not to delegate something that can be eliminated. If you need *your* boss's approval to eliminate a report or activity, explain to your boss that the payback does not justify the cost of continuing it.

Also, be careful not to rationalize hanging onto a job. Be honest with yourself. No one else need see these sheets. It's between you and yourself. Are you really hanging onto a job because it gives your ego a lift? Is there a certain amount of prestige attached to doing the job? Do you obtain visibility, recognition, acceptance? Or is it really a key activity that can only be performed at your level in the organization? At this stage, you should also question whether the time being spent on an activity can be reduced. Even time obligations can be performed more efficiently.

After you have completed the first three columns for all the activities, move on to the fourth. Can someone reporting to you actually do the job? This doesn't mean after going back to night school for three years. It means after a brief orientation period of a few days at the most. Is an employee able to *do* it? This is *assuming* he or she has the time and the desire to do it and you have the time and desire to teach. If the answer is "yes," record this in the column. If the answer is a definite "no," record this response instead.

Now, if the answer is "no," ask yourself another question. Can someone be *trained* to do it? Here again, training does not mean returning to university for a

Ph.D. in physics or undergoing a five-year management development program. But, if spending three or four hours each week for several months to personally train an employee will enable that person to take the job off your hands, the answer would be "yes." Record this in the column. If the answer is still "no," record this instead.

Move to the final column. Who on your staff do you have in mind for the job? If it could be done by more than one person, jot down all the names. Don't enter the same person's name for most of the activities simply because they could obviously do the best job. Delegation includes the process of training and development, and *all* your employees should be included in this process. You will have to balance the workload at the time the delegation actually takes place. It's not practical to assign everything to one person. However, if there is only one person who you feel has the education, background and capability necessary to be trained for the specific task in question, enter the one name only.

The development and training of people takes time initially. But the investment is well worth it when you see the results. A capable employee gets the job done faster, makes fewer errors and doesn't waste your time with incessant questions. For every hour spent in training, you will receive countless hours of good performance in return. Don't procrastinate. You'll be just as busy two months from now. Plan. Which skills need development? What's the best method of training your staff? Think it through. Then schedule the necessary time to get the tasks accomplished.

Don't spend all your time on those employees who obviously need training and neglect those top performers. If 20 percent of your employees produce 80 percent of the results (an extension of Pareto's Law), there's no doubt you should be developing that 80 percent of your employees to make them more effective. But look at it another way. Just think of the impact on the organization if those 20 percent were given a little extra help. For example, effective utilization of time is one area where *everyone* can improve, regardless of how effective they are already. Training is an ongoing process that requires constant reinforcement. Don't neglect your strongest people. A little training will result in a tremendous increase in effectiveness.

Also, beware that you don't fall into the trap of delegating most of the tasks to the same person. It is an easy trap to fall into because there's usually one person who is more willing, accurate and faster than the rest. But eventually that person becomes overloaded and ineffective. Or quits. Meanwhile, while the strong are getting stronger, the weak are getting weaker. You have a responsibility as a manager to develop *all* of your people. To ensure even distribution of the tasks, draw up a form similar to the one shown in Exhibit 12.In the left-hand column, list the parts of your job which you feel you can delegate. These can be taken from the sheets you prepared for Exhibit11.Along the top, list the people who report to you, and whose names you included in the last column of Exhibit 11.Then *plan* to delegate by assigning the tasks to these candidates, recording the amount of time each task will take, and the total time required on a monthly basis for all the tasks assigned to each person.

Once you know the approximate amount of time, you will have to determine how you are going to free up enough of the employees' time. It could be that they already *have* enough time available, but more than likely you will have to eliminate, combine, or reassign some of the jobs they are currently performing. The important thing is to make sure they are working on necessary activities, not trivial tasks.

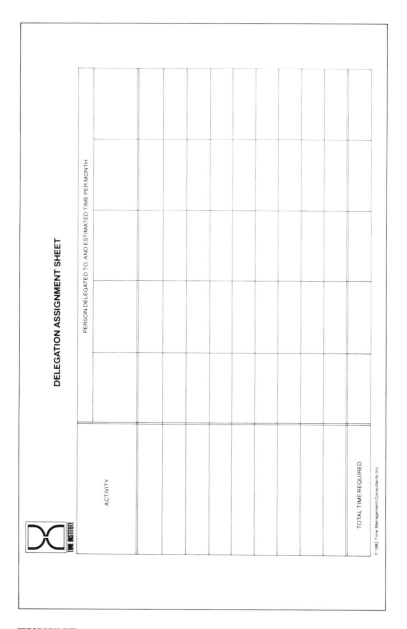

EXHIBIT 12

Delegation Assignment Sheet

CLARIFY YOUR ASSIGNMENTS

At the time you assign a task to an employee, make sure you provide all the information necessary for the completion of the task.

Never assume your employees have completely understood your explanation of the task. Provide details. Repeat information, talk slowly. If you rush through an explanation, the employee will assume that you feel it is easy, and doesn't merit a lengthy discussion. This in turn inhibits questions. Even if the employees don't understand, there is no way they are going to admit it and appear stupid. After all, they can always figure it out later. Or so they think!

Although it is important that people thoroughly understand what you say, don't insult their intelligence by asking them to repeat the information. This is an old practice and I feel a demeaning one. If you are in doubt about the effectiveness of your communication, use *yourself* as the patsy. Ask something like, "Oh, did I mention that we had to send a copy to purchasing?" They will likely respond, "Yes, you said the pink copy goes to purchasing, the yellow copy to receiving and the white copy to the supplier."

There are all kinds of questions you can ask to get feedback — all of them appearing to question *your* intelligence, not theirs. Such as, "I can't recall if I told you about the return policy...", or "There's something else I wanted to mention. Did I explain the..." As a manager, you have to shoulder as much responsibility as it takes. Remember, your job is to build up *their* self-confidence, not to build up their confidence in *you*.

Don't let your impatience show, even if you are impatient. Your job as a manager is to *communicate*, and communication hasn't taken place until the person *understands*. They will not be receptive if you criticize them, show impatience, disrespect, or in any way threaten their self-image.

Whenever you assign a task to one of your subordinates, be sure to outline the feedback expected. If you start imposing controls later on, your employee may feel you lack confidence in his or her ability.

Use the following checklist to ensure that you have explained the assignment clearly:

☐ Exact date the employee is to assume the new responsibility and the duration of this new assignment.
☐ The purpose of the task, and how it relates to the organization's goals.
☐ A detailed explanation of how the task is currently done — if, in fact, it is.
☐ A comment to the effect that you welcome any suggestions as to how the method can be improved.
☐ An explanation of the various resources and sources of information available to the employee should he or she encounter problems.
☐ A summary of the types of problems encountered in the past and how they were handled.
☐ An explanation of any unusual circumstances or problem areas that might arise in the future.
☐ The limits of the employee's authority. Which types of decisions are to be made by him or her and which ones have to go to a higher level of authority.
☐ Any new reporting relationships and lines of communication involved in the new assignment.
☐ The type and frequency of feedback expected.
☐ How the employee's performance will be evaluated.

It seems as though anything worthwhile is either expensive or difficult. Delegation is both. But its expense lies in the value of the time being spent in training and explaining, and this expense will soon be recovered. Its difficulty lies in the fact that most of us are impatient, and overly time conscious. The difficulty disappears once we learn to control ourselves — to recognize that it is the results, not activity, that determine our effectiveness.

Chapter Six

RELEASING YOUR JOB TO OTHERS

Let Your Employees Decide

The hardest part of delegation is letting go. Even though we have confidence in an individual and have explained the objective of the task, we frequently insist on being involved in the decision-making process.

"Janet, we just don't seem to have enough space in the office to store things. There are boxes of supplies on the floor behind desks, cabinets are jutting into the aisles, and piles of paper are stored on top of everything. The place is a mess. Would you look at the situation and figure out how we can arrange the furniture to accommodate some additional shelving, cabinets, files or whatever we need so we can make the office look presentable? You might contact a few office equipment suppliers to see what they have to offer in the way of movable files or portable shelving. But we can't afford to spend more than $2,000 on this."

So far so good. You have explained what it is you are trying to accomplish and why. You have set a guideline in terms of money that can be spent. And you have even offered a suggestion as to how Janet might start. And it's a good task to delegate. You could spend hours rearranging furniture, thumbing through catalogues, thinning out files and straightening out clutter. But your time is too valuable for that kind of nonsense. And this would be a challenge for Janet, who has not been given very much responsibility since recently being promoted to assistant office manager. You now have an opportunity to show confidence in her as your assistant. The office staff will view her as a person of some authority, and her visibility within the organization will be enhanced.

Unfortunately, you don't leave it at that. "For instance, Janet, I think this bank of filing cabinets should be moved against the back wall. Then there would be room for some closed-in shelving to accommodate all the letterhead boxes that are strewn about.

Get quotes from Jackson Shelving and Amalgamated Interiors on a floor to ceiling unit. Those boxes of old files on the tops of cabinets should be..."

Suddenly, you are not only telling her what you want accomplished, you are telling her step-by-step how to do it. You are forcing your ideas upon her, repressing her own creativity. After all, will she disagree with her boss, and suggest a better way? She might. But you're taking a chance. And if she does come out with "Wouldn't it be better if..." chances are you will jump to the defensive and start rationalizing as to why *your* suggestion is better. After all, you are the boss, and you have been office manager for eight years. It just wouldn't do to be outshone by the recent addition to your department.

You may not feel that insecure, and may readily accept her suggestions over your own once you assess the ideas objectively. But the point is, you have become *involved* in the decision-making process. And you will probably stay involved until the project is completed. Janet will continually bounce the various alternatives off you. "Bill, what do you think about moving the copier machine into the print shop?" Or, "Is it okay if we have some shelving built in the reception area?"

Can you afford the time? Can you afford Janet's dependency upon you that you are nuturing? Can you afford to do without the fresh ideas which could be stifled?

Let Janet complete the task on her own. This doesn't mean you should sit idly by while she chops up three desks for firewood and rips out two walls. But only intervene if actions jeopardize the success of the assignment. Be available to answer any questions she may have concerning the objectives of the task. But refrain from interjecting every day with your own ideas. Evaluate the results. They may not be the same results you would have obtained. They may be better.

Or they may be worse. The important thing is they are *her* results, achieved using her own ingenuity, common sense, and experience.

When you evaluate the results, start with the positives. Don't start with "Janet, the way you've arranged the shelving is going to interfere with deliveries..." Instead, start with the comment, "I like the way you have recessed the cabinets so they don't stick out like a sore thumb..." Be honest with your appraisal, but place emphasis on the good points. Delegation is a process of developing your employees. If they could already do what you do, as well as you do it, there would be no need to delegate. You could simply turn over your job to that person and move on to another position in the organization.

LET YOUR EMPLOYEES EXCEL

We are reluctant to admit that someone else can do a better job than we can, especially if that person reports to us and especially if that job is one that *we* held for ten years! But let's face it; once we delegate a job to someone else, from that point on we know less and less about the job, and our subordinates know more and more.

Don't try to remain the "expert" on a task that you have delegated. Don't look over your employee's shoulder offering advice or criticizing his or her method unless you sincerely feel that failure to intervene would cause a significant setback to the goal of the task.

There's little doubt that your employees will make

mistakes. And some of these mistakes may be costly. But compared to the value you will receive as the employees learn from their mistakes and continue to improve, the cost will be minimal. As the employees spend more and more time on the job, and you are involved less and less, your "interference" should decrease. Otherwise you risk saddling your employees with decisions that are inferior to their own. After all, will your decisions always be better, even after your subordinates have been working on the tasks longer than you have?

As a manager, you should recognize that you cannot do everything and still do it well. You must continually train your subordinates to take on greater responsibilities so that you, in turn, can replace those responsibilities with ones of even greater value to the organization. Once you have grown into a job, you should plan to grow out of it.

Managers must manage. And to manage is to accomplish significant results *through* other people. It is not a competitive sport to see who can do the better job. Nor is a manager meant to be the "great guru" with all the answers. It is not our job to impress our employees with our knowledge, or to consistently come through with the right decisions every time an employee falters. An effective leader is not one who simply earns his subordinates' confidence, but one who develops subordinates so that they gain confidence in *themselves*.

If you have made the objective of the job clear, trained the employee adequately, and encouraged him or her to change the method to more effectively attain the objective, eventually he or she should be doing the job better than you did. But make sure the employee is allowed to do things his or her own way as long as the quality of the job doesn't suffer. There is more than one way to accomplish something. Left to himself, an employee will usually find a better way. Recognize that effort. Encourage it. Reward it. Don't block it, resent it, or be jealous of it. A good manager does not necessarily do the best work; he or she encourages the employees to perform *their* best.

Let your employees excel.

Chapter Seven

GUIDELINES FOR DELEGATION

Recognize The Need To Delegate

Physicians have assistants to relieve them of paper-work and other routine activities so they can spend their time with patients. Other busy professionals also rely on assistants in the conduct of their practices.

So why not managers? If you are spending too much time on administrative detail and not enough time on the high-payoff priority activities, perhaps you need an assistant. But if you have one, make sure you delegate most of the non-managerial activities to him or her. As a manager, the bulk of your time should be spent planning, organizing, staffing, directing, controlling, innovating and representing your company. You shouldn't be spending your time answering routine letters and telephone calls, attending low priority meetings, or searching through filing cabinets for misplaced correspondence.

The general rule should be as follows:

A. If it's not necessary, eliminate it.
B. If it's necessary, but can be done by others, delegate it.
C. If it can't be delegated, and is critical to the attainment of your objective, do it yourself as effectively as possible.

Here are some specific guidelines to follow when delegating:

Know Your People

Before you start to delegate to anyone, it is imperative that you get to know your employees. Talk to them. Observe them, and above all, *listen* to them. What are their personal goals? What are their career plans? Where do they want to be within that organization one year, five years, ten years from now? Are they able to accept greater responsibility? Do they *want* any more responsibility? What are their needs? What motivates them? How do they feel about self-development?

Never assume that everyone wants more responsibility and wants to be promoted. Some of your staff may be frightened to death of it. Talk to them. Find out how they feel about taking on certain tasks and functions. Involve them at the "considering" stage. Don't make your decision arbitrarily and then thrust the new assignment onto them. You need their involvement if you want their commitment.

Take the Time to Communicate Clearly

Unnecessary interruptions are a waste of time. And they are frequently caused by poor communications. If you don't explain an assignment properly, your employees will have to interrupt you later for clarification. If you don't supply complete information, they will have to interrupt you to ask. Sometimes they might *not* interrupt you to ask — resulting in even greater time loss. They might postpone the task, take too long to do it, avoid it completely or do it incorrectly.

We sometimes communicate under stress. We're pressured, in a hurry, on the move. It pays to take the time to communicate clearly. An investment of time at the outset pays dividends later.

Be Specific When Giving Assignments

Whenever you assign a task to a subordinate, be sure to (a) get a commitment as to the expected completion date, (b) have a follow-up system to ensure commitments are honored, and (c) insist that any revisions to the due date are advised *in advance*, not on or after the due date.

In most cases, employees know well in advance that a due date cannot be met. That's the time they should advise you, so that you can make adjustments to *your* schedule. Don't accept excuses after the deadline has passed. Force your employees to plan. Once they get in the habit of planning and scheduling their activities, they won't have as much trouble meeting deadlines.

Delegate, Don't Abdicate

Dumping jobs onto your subordinates and then disappearing is not delegation — it's cutting your throat. Delegation must be planned. Consult with your employees first; select people you think are both capable of doing the job, and would like to do the job. Train them. Delegate gradually, insist on feedback, and *then* leave them alone. But leaving them alone does not mean ceasing to communicate.

Get in sync with people who report to you. Hold a daily five minute, stand-up meeting each morning. Compare notes. Discuss priorities. Make sure you all agree on the day's important objectives, and are aware of each other's schedule.

Accountability works both ways. Employees are accountable to the manager for the successful completion of delegated assignments. But managers are also responsible for adequate feedback — explaining to their employees why certain decisions were made and actions taken.

Watch What You Delegate

Don't delegate what you can eliminate. If it's not important enough for you to do personally, it may not be important enough for your people to do either. Respect their time and their ability. Don't waste it on nonproductive or unprofitable tasks. Your success can be multiplied a thousand times if you concentrate on the high-return jobs, and encourage your subordinates to do likewise — don't spoil it by using your people as a dumping ground for "garbage" jobs.

On the other hand, be careful not to delegate tasks that are critical to the success of the organization, can only be performed adequately at your level or above, and which you are expected to perform personally. Producing highly confidential information, conducting performance appraisals, and handling key customer accounts could be examples of this type of activity.

Delegate Important Tasks

Don't limit your delegation to those trivial, repetitive tasks which have very little impact on your organization's effectiveness. Some managers are reluctant to part with key jobs that have a high degree of visibility. They feel that these jobs are too important to be entrusted to their employees.

And yet there are some critical jobs with low visibility, such as collecting unpaid bills, which are entrusted to the other people. Selling is important, but a manager wouldn't think of doing it himself. Financial statements are important but the Vice-President of Finance would not think of keeping the books himself.

Delegation is *sharing* your job with the people who work for you. This includes the highly visible, important tasks as well as the routine.

Delegate Enjoyable Tasks

Delegate some of the things you *don't want* to delegate. We tend to hang on to the things we *like* doing, even when they interfere with more important tasks, and even though our subordinates could probably do them just as well. Share the interesting work with your employees. One of the most important advantages of effective delegation is the fact that it enriches your subordinates' jobs. Don't confine your delegation to the boring, repetitive tasks — look for the interesting ones first. If we get to like certain activities too much, we hate to part with them. Consequently, we spend time that could be better utilized on something else. It's great to like our jobs, but let's not fall in love with too many low pay-off activities. Consider delegating some of those pleasant tasks to others. They'll probably be just as enjoyable for them, perhaps more so. And you can use the time gained to take on more valuable jobs that earn a greater return on the time invested. And chances are, they will prove to be even *more* enjoyable.

Recognize that Everything Takes Time

There's no such thing as "spare time." Perhaps it had meaning at one point in the past. Perhaps employees had certain jobs to do, and when those were completed they had "spare time" to use as they pleased. But do you see anyone sitting around today wondering what to do with their "spare time"?

Don't insult your employees by asking them to do something in their "spare time" because it suggests they don't have enough meaningful work to fill their day. Ask them, instead, to *schedule* the job for completion by a specific date. This may involve some rescheduling on their part. Your higher priority task may displace some less important ones. Be prepared to discuss priorities with them. You may even end up changing the due dates on a few items.

But ask for something to be done in their "spare time," and you may never see that task completed.

Don't Always Delegate to the Most Capable Employees

Delegation is one of the most effective methods of developing your people. So don't continually delegate to the most capable ones, or they'll get stronger, while the weak get weaker. Take the extra effort to spread delegation across the board, and develop a strong team with no weak links.

Trust Your Subordinates

Delegation not only saves time, it develops your subordinates. But it frequently fails because managers are too willing to take a task back if it is not going well. Take the time to explain fully what is required of your employee, and then be willing to accept something less than you could do yourself. Don't oversupervise, allow a few mistakes, and be willing to let your employees develop at their own pace.

Be sure to delegate the authority, as well as the responsibility. Don't continually look over the delegatees' shoulders, interfere with their methods, or jump on them when they make a mistake. Be prepared to trade short-term errors for long-term results. Maintain control without stifling initiative.

Delegate the Objective, Not the Procedure

One of the bonuses you receive from effective delegation is that in many cases the job is done better in the hands of someone else. Don't resent it, encourage it. Delegate the whole task for specific *results*, de-emphasizing the actual *procedure*. Your subordinate, under less pressure, less harried, and with a fresh viewpoint, will likely improve upon the method you've been using. Review results, not the manner in which he or she arrived at them.

Force Your Employees to Plan

If you are continually being interrupted by people needing "instant approvals," take corrective action immediately. You cannot work effectively while responding to others. Rush jobs normally result from lack of planning. Don't suffer because of someone else's failure to schedule properly. Let it be known that you need two days' advance notice to peruse and approve reports, budgets, projects, etc. Leave some unscheduled time on your own planning calendar to accommodate these requests. But don't interrupt your previously scheduled priority task simply because they "need approval right away." They should have included the two-day approval time in *their* schedule. There will be exceptions, but keep them to a minimum. If you always acquiesce, you'll always be expected to.

Ask for Solutions, Not Problems

Resist the urge to answer questions posed concerning the delegated task. First, force the employees to think it through. Ask what they would suggest. Delegation has not taken place until employees are not only able to perform the job, but are able to *make the decision* that you alone used to make.

If you want to ensure that your employees think about the problems they encounter before bringing them to you to be resolved, post this sign on your door: "Please come in. But before you do, be sure that you have thought about the problem and are now prepared to recommend a solution."

Let Them Make a Few Mistakes

If you can review your own past year's performance and honestly say you didn't make any mistakes, it's time to be concerned. Every manager who innovates, introduces changes, delegates and makes significant decisions, makes mistakes. It goes with the job. If you never make mistakes, you're not managing, you're coasting.

Similarly, don't be afraid of letting your employees make mistakes. Encourage them to continually try something new and to take advantage of opportunities. Remember that good judgment is the outcome of experience, and experience is the outcome of bad judgment.

Give Credit, Absorb Blame

Once you have delegated a task, it is as though you were still doing it yourself as far as other people are concerned. You can't delegate *your* responsibility. So when someone calls to complain that the report is not as "professional" as it used to be, accept the criticism. Thank the person for pointing out the fact, and promise an improvement. But resist the urge to blame it on your employee. Act as a buffer; provide feedback to the employee in the form of suggestions for improvement rather than in the form of criticism and complaint.

But when someone calls to congratulate you on a fantastic job, be quick to point out that "Sam is doing that now." Delegate the credit, but not the blame. When "outsiders" start complimenting Sam directly, motivation is on the upswing.

Develop Your Employees

Are your employees approaching the limits of their potential or are they only performing at 20 percent of their potential? Unfortunately, not many get by on their natural ability, when they could actually increase that ability by learning and developing various skills related to their jobs.

When your employees set objectives for the next year, don't let them limit those objectives to quality and quantity and cost and production. Make sure there are some professional development goals there as well. Goals such as reading a certain number of books on specific topics, and attending a specific number of seminars. Encourage sound time management, physical fitness, and proper diet as well.

Bad leaders are the product of a lack of good training, and the absence of performance standards. Good leaders are made through constant upgrading in training to keep pace with changes, personal development, and proper evaluation against a high standard.

Chapter Eight

KEEPING TRACK OF ASSIGNMENTS

The Delegation Record

Almost everyone is prone to procrastination. And many of us are forgetful as well. So it's essential that you have a record of the various projects and tasks you have delegated to others, along with the promised completion dates.

Make up a Delegation Record similar to the one shown in Exhibit 13 with columns for the date the task was assigned, a brief description of the task, the date the task is due to be completed, the actual date that the task *was* completed, and comments about the quality of the completed job.

This form is not meant to be used for those projects of an ongoing nature which are spelled out in a job description, but only for those one-time assignments that you could easily lose track of. It's bad enough if an employee forgets or delays an assignment, but it's even worse if *you* forget about it. This form will not only keep you from forgetting to follow up — it will also eliminate the necessity of continually interrupting your employees throughout the day.

When you first think of the project or task to be assigned, record the day's date, and a few words about the task itself. Then continue your work until it's time to make the actual assignment. The normal impulse is to interrupt yourself and the employee right away so you won't forget. And it would probably be one of many such interruptions throughout the day. Instead, wait until you are ready to discuss it with your employee. Then *ask* him or her what a likely or possible completion date will be. Don't dictate a due date unless it is urgent; get a commitment from the employee instead. Record the agreed-upon date, and then leave the employee alone. But make sure the employee agrees in advance to adhere to a specific deadline. Insist that he or she notify you *in advance* if changing priorities indicate they will not be able to meet the deadlines as planned. Learning *after the fact* that a job was not completed is unaccept-

DELEGATE

DELEGATION RECORD

MANAGER _____ MONTH _____

Date Assigned	Assignment	Due Date	Date Completed	Comments

"INSTANT" TASKS   check box at right when completed

EXHIBIT 13
Delegation Record

90

DELEGATION RECORD

MANAGER _John Smith_   MONTH _May / 84_

Date Assigned	Assignment	Due Date	Date Completed	Comments
1st	Prepare proposal on plant expansion	5/28		
4th	Revise Rate card for magazine	5/17		
9th	Summarize Returns and allowances	5/11	5/6	
9th	Report on Management conference	5/24		
14th	Quote re: A.C.L. account	5/18		

"INSTANT" TASKS   check box at right when completed

- Call Jim re: June meeting	✓	- final production figures ?	
- Check grievance status	✓	- New desk rec'd yet ?	✓
- Reply to Johnson complaint	✓		
- Q.C. Report ?	✓		
- Date of staff meeting ?			
- Lunch Monday ?			

able. Knowing in advance will allow you to adjust your own schedule or juggle the employee's priorities so the job *does* get done on time.

If employees schedule the various assignments in their planning calendars, they will know in advance if a due date can or cannot be met.

The morning the job is due, make a follow-up call. Simply say, "John, I realize it's early yet, but I was wondering if you are going to have any trouble getting that 'XYZ' job to me today." John may have forgotten the job is due (although he'll rarely admit it) so your follow-up call will ensure the job is delivered on time. Don't wait until the deadline is passed; the purpose is to get the job done on time, not to chastise employees for *not* getting it done on time.

For more time-consuming assignments, you may want to follow up several days or weeks in advance. In this case, record the follow-up date as well as the due date on the Delegation Record. Each morning make it a habit of glancing at the form to see whether any follow-up calls are due that day.

Have a separate sheet for each person reporting to you. Keep these together in a binder and use a new sheet each month. Refer to these forms at performance appraisal time, and give credit for prompt and effective completion of assignments. You will usually remember the foul-ups, but it's much more difficult to recall all those assignments which were completed expeditiously without error.

The Delegation Record will also reveal whether you are distributing assignments evenly among your employees. You may be assigning the majority of tasks to one or two people without realizing it. It's easy to do if you have an employee who is eager to learn, never complains, always does a good job, and doesn't know when to say no. It's the path of least resistance. But, as mentioned earlier, you may so overwhelm a few employees with assignments, they end up developing health problems. Or they may simply quit.

The Instant Tasks section at the bottom of the Delegation Record provides space to record those minor assignments that can hardly be classed as delegation, such as: "Check the price of felt pens"; "Notify Bill Jackson his order is ready"; "How many valves are in stock?" etc. This is a "things to do" list for the people reporting to you, items that require little time and effort, few instructions or decisions, and which can be reported on almost immediately.

These are the types of assignments or questions that normally cause continual interruptions throughout the day. But instead of interrupting anyone, simply jot these "things to do" in the Instant Tasks section as they occur to you, and review them all at one sitting — say in the afternoon. The next day, during your regular five-minute meeting, you can review the previous day's assignments and check them off as they're completed.

Don't rely on your memory. It only takes a few seconds to record something. But it could save hours and dollars later.

ASSIGNMENT AND INFORMATION RECORD

In addition to making assignments, managers must keep their employees informed about decisions, policies, procedures, etc. which affect them. It's difficult to keep track of all this information as well as who was informed and who wasn't. It's frustrating, demoralizing, and costly when errors occur simply because the employee was not informed of a change.

The Assignment and Information Record, shown in Exhibit 14, may solve the problem. It combines the Delegation Record with a simple communications record.

Place the name of your subordinates (or the individuals you must keep informed) in the box at the top right of the form opposite the number 1, 2, 3, etc. You can add more numbers if more people are involved. When you think of a task that should be delegated, describe it briefly in the second column. Then check off the number in the third column which corresponds to the employee to whom you will be delegating.

When you talk to the employee, jot down the date in the first column. Get a commitment as to completion date and record it in the fourth column. Glance at this column every morning to see whether any projects are due. When completed, record the completion date in the last column.

To this point, it is being used as though it were a Delegation Record. But for information that must be communicated to several people (policies, procedures, decisions, etc.), follow this procedure: Put several checkmarks in column 3, corresponding with the individuals who should have the information. Put a cross through the checkmark when you inform these people. Write the date in the last column after everyone has been told. This last column is a flag. If it is blank it tells you there is still information to be communicated or that there are assignments due.

There is so much information that must be communicated, it is impractical to write memos covering everything. And people may not even read them. Yet forgetting to pass on information or overlooking someone not only wastes time later, it can cause morale problems and costly errors as well.

Try a form similar to the one described and see if it works for you. You may only want to use it for vital

Assignment and
Information Record

1 JOHN	4 SAM
2 MARY	5 JEAN
3 BILL	6

Date	Assignment or information to be communicated	ASSIGNED TO: 1	2	3	4	5	6	Due Date	Date completed and comments
5/2	New procedure re: employee purchases	✓	✓	✓	✓	✓			5/2
5/4	Plant shutdown dates July 1-18	✓		✓					5/5
5/14	Revise procedure re: petty cash				✓			5/25	5/24
5/14	New price list effective July 1st	✓		✓		✓			5/15
5/16	Submit holiday requests	✓	✓	✓	✓	✓		5/28	
5/17	Feedback from president re: Frankfurt	✓	✓	✓	✓	✓			5/25

EXHIBIT 14

Assignment and Information Record

information that could have a major impact on the organization. Or you may want to use it for *everything*, including those ideas you get while working on something else. Jot them down while they're fresh in your mind, and decide who to delegate them to later. You may want to include your own name on the form, and carry out some of those creative ideas yourself.

It is very easy to get sidetracked while working on priority projects simply because we suddenly recall some information that has to be communicated or a task that has to be assigned. By having a Delegation Record or an Assignment and Information Record at hand, we are able to resist the impulse to interrupt ourselves and others, quickly jot down the item on the sheet, and resume working without having to reorient ourselves to the task at hand.

Chapter Nine

CONTROLLING PERFORMANCE

Communicate After You Delegate

Assuming you have several employees, and have delegated to them all, how do you distribute your time among them? Many managers find they spend excessive amounts of time with one or two employees, neglecting the others. This is an easy trap to fall into. After all, some employees are more pleasant to be with. They are cheerful and positive and cooperative. Others may tend to complain a lot, idle time away over coffee, or be unjustly critical. It's only natural to want to spend more time with those employees who have a good attitude. But are they the ones who need you the most?

Similarly, you may be delegating jobs you tended to enjoy, and still love to be involved in, to those employees you favor. Those interesting, challenging tasks which stimulate creativity, perhaps the ones you were reluctant to give up. Or those familiar tasks which you performed for years and years; the ones you could perform blindfolded; the ones in which you excelled. Your time will not be shared equally among your people.

You must be careful not to oversupervise some employees and neglect others. Maintain a balance. Make yourself available to all employees without interfering with their decisions. Offer guidance, inspiration and encouragement. People appreciate a boss who is interested in them, who is accessible to them, and who has confidence in them.

You may think you are dividing your time evenly among your employees when you are not. Time is deceiving. If you kept a record, you might be surprised as to how little time you do spend with certain employees. Most of your time with respect to them may be spent sending memos or messages. Don't hide behind paperwork. Management is a people business, not a paperwork business. If a personal visit is impossible, use the telephone. And keep your priorities straight; show concern for the person first, the job second. If it weren't for people there wouldn't be any jobs.

If you want to check yourself, draw up a few sheets similar to the one shown in Exhibit 15, the Weekly Communication Record. Keep it in an obvious spot on your desk and, each afternoon, quickly jot down the type of communications, if any, you have had with each employee that day. If you haven't contacted them, leave the spaces blank. Mark in a T for telephone calls, P for personal visits, M for memos, letters or other written messages. Examine the record each week to see if there is any trend. Do you tend to communicate more frequently with certain individuals? Do you communicate only by memos or telephone calls? Are some people being ignored? Are some people being overwhelmed with calls, visits and memos? Then ask yourself why. Is it because of lack of confidence in an employee? Do you enjoy being with certain people? Are you more familiar with certain jobs? Is it convenience of location? Or does it just "happen" that way?

Then make a conscious effort to distribute your contacts evenly among all employees and see how the Weekly Communication Record changes.

There is a school of thought that suggests that managers should not have to go near their supervisors once proper delegation has taken place. This is supposed to indicate confidence in employees, and a recognition that they don't need watching. The supervisors' sense of achievement and recognition supposedly comes from the fact that they know they are doing a good job. They are looked upon as "entrepreneurs" in charge of their own little "companies" within a company.

Well, having been an entrepreneur for over fifteen years, I can testify that it is a pretty lonely job sometimes. We all need personal contact, encouragement and reassurance and there is a difference between

M = Memo P = Personal Visit T = Telephone Call	**Supervisors**				
	Jack	Sally	Bill	Tom	Sue
Monday	M/P	M	P	M	
Tuesday	M/T				P
Wednesday	P/T	T		M	
Thursday	T		P	M	M
Friday	M/P/T	M/P		T	M/T

EXHIBIT 15

Weekly Communication Record

leaving our employees alone in respect to their decision-making and *leaving them alone.* To maintain personal contact does not entail job interference. It entails interpersonal relationships.

A common complaint of managers is that people take up too much of their time. How can they possibly get anything done if they spend so much time on their employees? And yet, if they are managers, that's how they should be getting things done — through their employees. Perhaps those managers are *doing* instead of *delegating.* By spending time with employees — by training, directing, motivating, evaluating, correcting and rewarding — managers are doing what they should be doing. Never begrudge the time spent with employees; it is time well spent.

KEEP EXPECTATIONS HIGH

You have probably heard about the experiment where average students were introduced to a teacher as hand-picked, high I.Q. students. The teacher was told that these particular students could be expected to show dramatic improvements over the course of the school year. And since the teacher expected great things from these "special" students, they received great things. The students improved remarkably.

It's the old self-fulfilling prophecy at work: Expect little and you'll get little; expect much and you'll get much. It's true in business as well as in school. If you label your employees as incompetent, and not worth the time to train, they won't disappoint you. But if you approach your employees as though they are hand-picked, high I.Q. people who are capable of achieving great things, you will have a completely different caliber of employee on your staff.

Always assume you have superior employees. And when things go wrong, look to *yourself* for the reason. Did you explain the situation properly? Did you rush through the instructions? Did you forget to warn the employee about those exceptional circumstances that might occur? Did you take certain knowledge for granted? Were your instructions ambiguous?

If you find yourself blameless, then there's only one possible answer. Even clever, superior employees slip up once in a while. It might even have happened to you on occasion. So see it as it is — an honest error that could have happened to anyone. Don't get upset, point the blame, or berate the employee. Nothing you can do now can turn back the clock and prevent the error from happening. It's already happened. But you *can* help prevent the same error from recurring. You *can* make it a learning experience for the employee. And you *can* protect the employee's self-esteem. How? By condemning the error, but not the person who made it.

Always give your employees the benefit of the doubt. Few employees would make a mistake on purpose. And when they do make a mistake, their self-image suffers. What they need at this point is not your criticism, but your assurance. Help build up their self-confidence. Let them know that you're not blaming them for the mistake. That it could have happened to anyone. Then ask them if they have any suggestions as to "how we can reduce the chances of this happening again?"

People learn from their mistakes. *What* they learn is up to you. They could learn that making mistakes is painful and demeaning and that they shouldn't take risks. And that if they do make an error they should try to bury it so they don't get raked over the coals. Or they could learn that to err is human and the name of the game is to make as few mistakes as possible, to learn from the mistakes that do occur, and to continue to strive to be creative and innovative.

Assume your employees are a hand-picked group of clever, creative, dedicated individuals. And eventually you may prove yourself to be right.

PERFORMANCE APPRAISALS

As a manager, your effectiveness depends upon how well your subordinates perform their delegated responsibilities. And for them to perform adequately, they must have constant feedback on how they are doing and what they can do to increase their effectiveness.

Thus the need for performance appraisals. Not only do formalized performance appraisals provide feedback and set the stage for personal development, they provide information on which salary increases and promotions can be based.

I say "formalized" since many managers claim they don't need a formal review. They are constantly providing feedback and counsel on a day-to-day basis. This can hardly be labeled a performance review, and managers who claim it is frequently have employees who claim they're never told where they stand.

A performance review is a two-way process. Employees should be given advance notice, have an opportunity to rate themselves, exchange information and ideas, clear up areas of disagreement or misunderstanding and participate in goal-setting for the future.

Unless you set aside a definite time for this review, chances are it will never take place, especially if performance has been less than desirable. We all hate to be the bearer of bad news and the tendency to procrastinate is increased.

This does not mean we should not provide daily feedback. On the contrary, the idea of withholding comment on incidents of poor or good behavior until the annual review is ridiculous. Your employee may have quit long ago. Or if not, the impact of criticizing or praising behavior of several months before would be minimal.

The old adage of providing immediate feedback on employee behavior still holds true. There should be no real surprises at review time.

The fact that you have set a predetermined time for an annual or semi-annual review forces you to provide meaningful feedback throughout the year — which in turn culminates in the year-end review. This review formalizes the process and sets the stage for goal-setting and personal development.

Appraisal forms should be kept simple. They only serve the purpose of insuring that a review has taken place and that the information is recorded. Resist rating personality traits. It's ridiculous to attempt to differentiate between "excellent" affability and "above average" affability. It does nothing to explain the affect this has had on performance or to help in correcting a fault.

Instead, the appraisal discussion should revolve around an evaluation of results achieved versus the goals previously established mutually by the subordinate and yourself. Don't forget to evaluate *how* these goals were achieved. Goals achieved at the expense of morale, creativity, or company reputation in the marketplace can hardly be indicative of superior performance.

When setting goals for the next year, don't be restricted to one-year goals. New goals might have completion dates of only a few months and others may go beyond one year. The tendency is to have goal-setting, performance reviews and salary increases all coinciding. This is not always wise.

Performance appraisals and salary increases should never be covered in the same meeting. Once salary is mentioned, it's difficult for an employee to concentrate on anything else. Two or three meetings should be scheduled. In the latter case, the first meeting would involve the evaluation of results achieved and goal-setting for the next year. The second meeting might focus on plans for personal development. The final meeting would then discuss salary adjustments for the ensuing year.

Regardless of the format or the forms used, the important thing about performance appraisals is to *have* them — and at regular intervals and with advance notice to the employees so they are not caught off-guard.

People like to know where they stand in the eyes of the boss. They can't be expected to improve their effectiveness if they have no criteria against which to compare their present level of competence or effectiveness.

And *their* effectiveness is *your* effectiveness — since, through delegated responsibilities, they are doing parts of *your* job.

Chapter Ten

DEVELOPING YOUR PEOPLE

Communicate Through Strengths

"By the time I get a person trained properly, he quits!" How often have you heard that excuse for not developing people? People do quit at times. But if we don't train our people, and they stay with us forever, what kind of organization are we building? If a baseball coach kept the same unskilled, untrained players on the team, he'd never win a pennant. All companies have turnover. All companies lose good managers. Yet they must continually develop new ones to replace those who leave.

And what is the reason employees quit? If they are trained for greater things and never experience those greater things, they will become frustrated and leave. You must delegate enough challenging tasks to keep pace with their expanding abilities.

It can be discouraging to lose good employees after investing time, effort and money in training them. But you cannot afford the alternative. It is better to have highly motivated, skilled employees with you for two years, then unmotivated, mediocre employees with you for twenty.

You can provide your employees with the necessary on-the-job training, and can recommend outside courses and seminars to upgrade their technical skills. But you really can't *develop* people. What you *can* do is provide an environment that encourages them to develop themselves. To do this, be sure to emphasize your employees' strengths, not their weaknesses.

Many managers attempt to strike a responsive chord in their subordinates by zeroing in on their weaknesses. They use the "sandwich" technique of performance appraisal in which they will set an employee at ease with some favorable comment about his or her performance, and then discuss perceived failings and weaknesses at length. Finally, they close with a few more positive comments about the employee's performance so as not to leave a bitter taste in his or her mouth when the interview's over.

The emphasis is on the *middle* of the sandwich — the areas in which the employee did not excel, the goals he or she failed to reach, the undesirable behavior, the skills needing improvement, the rough edges of the employee's personality that need polishing, etc. The objective of the interview is to improve performance by detailing failings and suggesting corrective action for the future.

Unfortunately, improved performance doesn't necessarily result from such a technique. As long as the manager dwells on negatives, positive reinforcement is impossible, and behavior won't change. Instead, the employee jumps to his or her own defence, tries to rationalize the failures, poor performance and missed targets — and pays little heed to the remedial measures suggested by the manager. Criticism, constructive or otherwise, stifles communication.

Instead, the emphasis should be on the positive aspects of the employee's performance: the strengths, predominant skills, goals reached, potential exhibited. This emphasis should be carried throughout the entire interview. The manager should be *aware* of the employee's weaknesses, but should communicate through his or her strengths. The weaknesses and failures are not to be ignored during the interview, but they will surface naturally during the discussion of strengths. Most employees will *want* to correct any weaknesses that appear to be hindering their performance — *if* they receive sufficient recognition for their performance.

When communicating with your employees, remember to view each job as important and each person as important. View mistakes in a positive light, as a learning experience, not as a sign of inadequacy. Concentrate on positive signs. Expect a lot from your employees and chances are they will meet or surpass your expectations in return.

MOTIVATE YOUR PEOPLE

There are more theories of motivation than there are managers to practice them, but most of them have at least a few factors in common: (a) you can't "motivate" people, they motivate themselves; (b) behavior is goal-oriented; and (c) no two people will react exactly the same way in a given situation.

I'm sure there is no doubt in our minds that people are motivated *all of the time*. Some are motivated to increase their output, break sales records, and further the aims of the company, while others are motivated to goof off, cause friction among employees, and torpedo the boss. No doubt their behavior makes sense to them whether it makes sense to the rest of the world or not.

Other motivators could be accomplishing some goal or objective. It may be to increase earnings, land a promotion or gain a sense of achievement. Or it may be to escape boredom, attract attention, or relieve a sense of guilt!

People behave differently, and have different goals, depending on such factors as age, position, job satisfaction, home situation, and financial status. We have to recognize that people are individuals with different needs and it would be a mistake to treat everyone alike. What motivates one person to excel may not be acceptable or of consequence to the next.

The most important factor in motivation, then, is to *know your people*. What are their personal goals? Where are they on Maslow's "hierarchy of needs"? What is important to *them*? It is unrealistic to assume that your employees are not motivated by money. It is equally unrealistic to assume that your employees *are* motivated by money. With either assumption you would only be right part of the time. You cannot discuss the needs (or motivations) of people, only of *individuals*, since we all differ. And our needs may be different today than they were a year ago.

Man is goal-oriented. We all have personal goals whether we realize it or not. And now, more than ever before, people are formalizing their goals in writing — as witnessed by the proliferation of workshops available on career life planning and personal goal-setting.

Our culture has changed. People are no longer imbued with the work ethic. Work is no longer the be all and end all — it is simply a means to an end (or objective). The objective is the individual's personal goals.

To be truly motivated, a person's job (and the working environment) must offer accomplishment that leads to self-satisfaction and helps that person in the attainment of his or her personal objectives.

So find out where your people stand. Talk to them, observe them and above all *listen to them*. If their goals are compatible with those of the organization, great. And if their personal goals are being achieved through the job they are performing within the organization, terrific!

But if they are unhappy, you either have to change the job or change the person. In this instance no amount of "human relations" or salary increases or incentives will motivate that person (unless the employee decides to change his or her personal goals).

In a way, the old adage of "matching people with jobs" still holds true. The job itself, and the concomitant factors such as challenge, sense of achievement — or whatever turns the person on — available through the job are the most important factors in motivation.

Select people carefully. Be aware of their needs, and delegate jobs which provide results compatible with their personal goals. Provide sufficient extrinsic rewards such as salary, fringe benefits, recognition, etc., to satisfy *their* requirements.

And then, to help them motivate themselves, leave them alone. Guide them. Help them. But don't stifle them.

Chapter Eleven

ADVICE FOR THE DELEGATEE

What To Do If Your Boss Won't Delegate

Delegation is not only a great timesaver, it is a people-developer. Nothing develops decision-making ability and promotability more than taking on greater responsibilities along with the authority to carry them out. But you cannot always assume your boss will delegate to you. If your boss fails to delegate, take the initiative and explain that you are ready for more responsibility. Make suggestions as to the jobs you feel you will be capable of handling if provided with adequate training. In fact, there may be jobs you are capable of handling now, *without* any training.

Don't just sit back and wait for things to happen. If you *want* added responsibility and authority, you may have to ask for it. Some managers are reluctant to delegate, for a variety of reasons already discussed ranging from "no time to train" to "my people are too busy as it is." We're all human and subject to error, no matter where we sit on the organization's chart. So assume your boss has a problem delegating and help him or her out.

Why bother? Because it's *your* career that's being stifled. If you know very little about your boss's job and have had no experience handling problems and participating in decision-making at the level above you, your chances of promotion are greatly diminished.

Management is a team effort: no manager can operate effectively in isolation. You must learn all you can about your boss's job. Suggest activities or decisions that you might be able to take over, freeing him or her for more important activities. But do it with finesse: don't be pushy, as though you're power hungry or after the boss's job. Your immediate motive is to make the boss more effective by taking on more of the minor responsibilities. The more effective our bosses become, the greater the chances of them being promoted — making room for *our* promotion in return.

Don't count on *your* effectiveness standing out like glistening crystal against the dull performance of your boss. He or she can make you look bad — or good. You're in it together as a team. And it's easier to push someone up the ladder ahead of you than to scramble from beneath the weight of a fallen body.

But before you even approach the boss, make sure you have done your "homework." First of all, do you have a list of personal goals? This is vital, since you will want to take on those responsibilities which will contribute to the attainment of these goals. For instance, you shouldn't take on technical jobs if your goal is to become a general manager. Or you shouldn't assume responsibilities that would necessitate evening work if it would conflict with an evening course or family time. The tasks you assume should be compatible with your goals.

Next, take a look at your present job to ensure that you don't take on more tasks than you can handle effectively. Are there some low pay-off activities that you can eliminate? Can some jobs be transferred to someone else? It would be a good idea to jot down all the activities you perform on a regular basis, along with the approximate time spent on them. Question everything you do. Your time is too valuable to be wasted on trivial items.

When you assume new jobs, don't hesitate to suggest alternative ways of doing them. In order to do this, however, you must know the purpose of the job — what it is that you are trying to accomplish. When assigning jobs, the boss may explain the *procedure*, but not the results expected. Make sure you understand the *reason* the task is being performed.

Don't try to turn the world upside down all at once. Too many suggested changes too soon may threaten the boss and create resistance. After all, he or she may not like the inference that many of the tasks could have been performed better using other methods. It might be a good idea to follow the traditional procedure until you're sure of what you're doing. Then introduce the suggested changes gradually.

Be sure to clarify the type and frequency of feedback expected and the limit of your authority. Don't assume anything. One of the main reasons for *not* delegating is the lack of time for proper communication and training, so chances are the boss will not spend enough time during the delegation process. It's up to *you* to make sure you have all the information necessary.

When a problem arises, think about it before rushing to the boss for advice. What would *you* do if *you* were the boss? Then go to the boss with suggestions for solutions instead of leaving all the decision-making to the boss. Don't waste time mulling over the problem for days, however. If you need advice, ask. But there are other sources besides your boss. Cultivate a network of friends and business associates and don't hesitate to call on them. Some of us have an innate reluctance to ask for anything. We'd rather search for a street than stop at a service station to ask directions. We'd sooner waste ten minutes looking for a product than ask a store attendant where it's kept. And we would even search for items in our home before asking our spouse or children if they knew where they were.

Our tendency to be independent wastes time. If you need information, ask. Utilize other people's knowledge and experience. Build up a list of contacts. Meet as many people as possible at association meetings or conferences. And don't be afraid to ask their advice and utilize their knowledge.

Also, make sure you hand in completed tasks. Half-finished reports or outlines handed to the boss for comment are rarely appreciated. After all, that's why *you* got the job — to relieve pressure resting on his or her shoulders.

If you want to develop yourself *and* your career, you may have to take the initiative. By doing so, you are helping the organization as well. If you find yourself with a boss who refuses to delegate *regardless*, you have a decision to make. Either be happy with the level you have attained, or move to another organization.

HOW TO GET EXPERIENCE

There's an old saying that when a man with experience deals with a man who has money, the man with experience ends up with the money and the man who had the money ends up with experience.

Acquiring experience is a valuable learning process. Or at least it *can* be. But some individuals feel experience means simply putting in time. Others find they have the same experiences over and over again. How can we insure that we gain the kind of experience that will lead to self-improvement, career development and personal success?

The key is in taking control of our lives. We must decide what we want out of life, and *plan* experiences that will lead us to those goals.

Don't be satisfied just to drift through life, waiting for opportunities to present themselves. That's a copout. You're simply letting others determine what you will do and when you will do it. Take the responsibility for what happens to you. Then make it happen.

Regardless of what your goals are, it's experience that will see you attain them. And there's more to experience than achieving seniority. You must actively follow creative and educational pursuits. Listen to people. Talk to people. Participate. Observe. But don't just sit and absorb. One of the best ways of gaining experience from the standpoint of a return on invested time is to read. By reading you are exposed to the distilled experiences of hundreds of others — their most creative ideas, profound thoughts and valuable suggestions. By reading books related to your chosen field you can gain in one year what it would take ten years to accumulate by putting in time. And reading is not a passive activity — it is an active one. You must search out new ideas and information. Lift them from the pages. Summarize them on index cards. Utilize them in your own life. It's not the experience itself that leads to self-development, it's what you *do* with that experience.

Create a plan to improve yourself by reading on a regular basis. Set aside a definite period each day to read about a subject that interests you — that relates to your lifetime goals. The deeper you delve into a subject the more interested you will become. And one subject may lead to other subjects.

The other key method of gaining valuable experience involves interaction with people. If you don't like people, your experience will always be limited. Cultivate an interest in others. Ask questions. Discuss. Debate. Take advantage of any opportunity to find out more about your business friends, associates and competitors. Spend more time listening than talking. Discover how they have solved a problem you are facing, or how they solved one you *might* face in the future. Be on the lookout for more contacts. Meet as many people as you can. Don't rely on your memory — list their names, occupations and interests in a "contacts" book for future reference. Never sit idle while the world revolves around you. Participate at meetings, social events, and in educational classes. Be a front-seater. You have to work hard to get experience. It doesn't come to you on a silver platter. Sometimes the most successful people are those who are too busy to notice.

I'm not suggesting you work ten hours per day seven days per week. Or that you even extend the hours you're now working. But I am suggesting that you use the time you're presently devoting to your career as effectively as possible. Read, observe and listen *actively*.

Be prepared to handle the delegated authority and responsibility which will soon be yours. And it will be yours, if top management feels you are qualified. If you have the necessary experience.

To succeed at anything, you need desire, determination, and experience — the know-how — to make it all happen. Don't wait for experiences to find you. You find *them*.

EXCEL IN YOUR PRESENT JOB

It's okay to be future-oriented, but don't be so future-oriented that you ignore the present. Sometimes employees take courses to prepare themselves for advancement before they fully master the jobs they're in. Excel in what you do. Always do a better job than the position requires. Take courses, read books, attend seminars related to your field. You will soon be so skilled, knowledgeable and proficient at what you do that you will force yourself into a higher position — if not with your present company, then with a different one.

You will never be fully trained for a higher level job until after you get that job. Then you will grow into it quickly through actual experience, reinforced by the confidence you gained in having excelled in your previous job, and complemented by training directed at this new level.

There's a danger in advancing too quickly. It is important that you build up self-confidence and a strong self-image before taking on a complete set of new responsibilities. Otherwise you may fall victim to Lawrence Peter's "Peter Principle" and find yourself at your level of incompetence.

In a way, it's similar to high school. If you have not fully understood grade-nine mathematics, promotion to the next grade will cause you even more confusion and you will not only fail mathematics, but perhaps the subjects which require mathematics or for which mathematics is an asset.

Be prepared to grow into a job, and then out of it, but don't underestimate the time it takes to grow into it. This time can be reduced if your boss is an effective delegator. It can also be reduced if you accept the responsibility for developing yourself.

Chapter Twelve

DELEGATE OR STAGNATE

Building A Strong Future

A responsibility of every person on this earth is to pass along to the next generation as much of his or her acquired knowledge as possible. If the lessons learned and information acquired through experience, education and training were to be buried with each one of us, what a loss to humanity! Each of us experiences life differently. If we were to isolate ourselves from everyone else, we would remain ignorant. We must pool our knowledge, add it to the rapidly expanding body of knowledge already accumulated, and make it available as a resource for the generations to follow.

We pass along information and know-how to our children by instinct. We teach, train, coach continuously in an environment of love. We delegate every day of the week. We are patient through their early years when they are immature, uncoordinated, inexperienced. We have faith in them. We realize that one day they will mature, and that the rate at which they do mature and become self-reliant will largely depend upon how diligent we are in our role as parents.

In our role as managers we should approach our jobs with the same measures of diligence, patience and understanding. We must be willing to nurture our employees to maturity in respect to the jobs that we delegate to them.

Just as the world builds on the knowledge passed down from generation to generation, so an organization relies on the knowledge passed down from incumbent to incumbent. An organization cannot grow if its members operate in isolation, jealously guarding their knowledge and know-how and taking their skills with them upon promotion or upon retirement. Each of us has a responsibility to delegate — to share our knowledge and experience with those who report to us. This knowledge and experience, combined with their own, will produce even better managers to replace us as we fade from the scene. Our goal is not to look good ourselves, but to develop greatness in others. A football coach does not have to score touchdowns himself to win games.

Delegation must take place at all levels within an organization. If the president delegates and the vice-presidents don't, growth is stunted. The vice-presidents will be overworked and ineffective; the managers will be frustrated and confused; the employees will be unmotivated and unhappy. Delegation is the life-blood of any organization. Authority and responsibility must flow from the top to the bottom, circulating among the members of the organization like blood circulates through the body. To cut off the circulation, at any point, causes problems below.

Delegation is a simple process; but carrying out that process is difficult because people are not naturally inclined to give away a part of themselves. Delegation requires that we share our skills, knowledge, experience — our uniqueness — with others. And then give them a part of our job to boot. This is asking a lot. Yet we must realize that we, in turn, receive a part of someone else's uniqueness — and job. The final payoff is a strong organization consisting of the integrated talents and experiences of every individual member of that organization. And the total effectiveness is greater than the sum of the parts.

We can no longer afford the luxury of even a few individualists working in isolation from the rest of the organization. Business is in the big league now. Technological know-how, managerial skills, product quality, manufacturing capabilities and marketing techniques are at a new high. Competition is keen. The economic climate is unstable. Only the strong organizations will survive. And strength is not in the individuals, but in the team. Put a group of superstars together on any team, whether baseball, hockey, football or soccer, and they will still lose if they operate as individual superstars. But once they start operating as a team they become unbeatable.

Without delegation, small businesses remain small, unprofitable businesses remain unprofitable, mediocre employees remain mediocre. The success of any organization rests with you, the manager.

Delegate, or stagnate.